TATTERED TRUST

Ministry for the Third Millennium

TATTERED TRUST

Is There Hope for Your Denomination?

LYLE E. SCHALLER

ABINGDON PRESS / Nashville

TATTERED TRUST
Is There Hope for Your Denomination?

Copyright © 1996 by Abingdon Press

Library of Congress Cataloging-in-Publication Data

Schaller, Lyle E.
    Tattered Trust: is there hope for your denomination / Lyle E. Schaller.
      p.   cm.—(Ministry for the third millennium)
    ISBN 0-687-05740-X (pbk. : alk. paper)
     1. Protestant churches—North America.   2. Church renewal—Protestant churches.   3. North America—Religious life and customs.
    I. Title.   II. Series.
    BR510.S33   1996
    280'.4'0973—dc20
                                        96-32846
                                         CIP

Unless otherwise noted, Scripture quotations are from the New Revised Standard Version Bible. Copyright 1989 by the Division of Christian Education of the National Council of the Churches of Christ in the USA. Used by permission.

96 97 98 99 00 01 02 03 04 05 — 10 9 8 7 6 5 4 3 2 1

MANUFACTURED IN THE UNITED STATES OF AMERICA

To
Lynda and Scott

"And no one puts new wine into old wineskins; otherwise, the wine will burst the skins, and the wine is lost, and so are the skins; but one puts new wine into fresh wineskins."

Mark 2:22

CONTENTS

Contents

INTRODUCTION

What is this book about? First of all, it is about the need for initiating and responsible leadership.

In a recent book review Warren Bennis declared that "Around the globe, humanity currently faces three extraordinary threats: the threat of annihilation as a result of nuclear accident or war, the threat of a worldwide plague or ecological catastrophe, and a deepening leadership crisis in most of our institutions."[1]

Among the institutions threatened by this leadership crisis is the Christian church in North America.

Second, it is about the normal, natural, and predictable tendency for aging institutions to become self-centered, obsolete, and irrelevant to the needs and expectations of new generations. In other words, this book is about the need for new wineskins to carry the gospel into the new millennium to new generations of American-born residents and to recent immigrants.

Third, it is about living with the consequences of earlier decisions. Nineteenth-century Protestantism was marked by dozens of schisms and splits as dissidents left to create new denominations. From 1917 through 1988 the twentieth century was marked by a series of denominational reunions and mergers.

One example was the creation of the United Church of Canada in 1925. South of the border life was more complicated and produced a series of mergers. Lutherans can look back to 1917, 1918, 1930, 1960, 1962, 1963, and 1987 as significant merger dates. The United Methodist Church is a product of mergers and reunions dated 1922, 1939, 1946, and 1968. The Presbyterian Church (U.S.A.) is a product of the mergers and reunions of 1906, 1920, 1958, and 1983. The United Church of Christ is a product of mergers of 1931, 1934, and 1957. The Wesleyan Church is the product of a 1968 merger. The Evangelical Methodist Church is the product of mergers in 1960 and 1962. It would be easy to list another two dozen denominational mergers of the twentieth century.

This book is about the stresses and strains created when efforts are made to blend several different strands of culture, polity, doctrine, and practices into one new religious tradition called a denomination.

This book is about a concept detested by many in the ecumenical movement. One thread in this narrative is based on the conviction that the competition among the churches for new members is at an all-time high. Competition does produce "winners and losers in our religious economy," to quote the subtitle of a provocative interpretation of American church history.[2] Competition also can provide useful lessons for those who are open to learning from the competitors.

This book also is about a widely discussed quality in American culture called "trust." Should denominational structures for the twenty-first century be built on a foundation of trust? Or of distrust?

This book also is about the earthquakes that are flattening hierarchical structures all across our society.

This book is about money. What will be the sources for financing denominational systems in the new millennium?

This book is about the consequences of death. One consequence of death is that most of today's church members and leaders will be dead before the end of the first century of the new millennium. What are the most effective ways to reach younger generations and recent immigrants with the gospel of Jesus Christ?

Most of all, however, this book is about creating denominational systems that will be supportive of the life, ministry, and outreach of worshiping communities, both existing and those yet to be founded.

This book was written with the conviction that the old ways of doing church will not be adequate for ministry in the new millennium. The first chapter discusses a few of the consequences and victims of the earthquakes that have been shaking denominational and congregational foundations.

One victim could be the traditional denominational systems. The second chapter begins by describing a few of the consequences of this earthquake for congregations and goes on to suggest why congregational leaders should be concerned about the health, vitality, and future of their denominational system. In other words, this book is written by a denominationalist who is convinced regional and national denominational structures are legitimate orders of God's creation.

The third chapter elaborates on the conviction that we can learn from how competitors do church, and several of those lessons are described.

The future of your denominational system will be shaped by several fork-in-the-road decisions that are being made now and will be implemented in the years ahead. Ten of these fork-in-the-road choices are identified in the fourth chapter.

Those designing ministries and structures for the future need to pause once in a while and ask, "What's it all about?" A brief fifth chapter responds to that question from this observer's perspective.

Should the denominational structure determine the strategies that will be designed to reach younger generations and new immigrants? Or should the strategies be a product of the structure? The sixth chapter describes a dozen widely used strategies.

No good deed goes unpunished and every dream has a price tag on it. The seventh chapter reviews a few of the trade-offs that go with the dream of creating multigenerational, multicultural, and theological inclusive denominations.

How do you get there from here? That requires (1) a definition of "there," (2) agreement on where "here" is, and (3) the choice of the path that runs from here to there. The eighth chapter offers a case study in the use of trends to describe a piece of contemporary reality in one denomination. The tables in the appendix are included for those who want to collect comparable data for their denomination.

This observer has long been convinced that a key to shaping the future is asking the right questions. The ninth chapter offers two dozen questions that may be of value for the task force charged with redesigning your denominational system.

Finally, a useful congregational planning model is to identify five to fifteen different scenarios for the future. This can stimulate members' creativity as they plan for the future. Instead of asking the blank sheet of paper question, "What do you believe God is asking of this congregation in the years ahead?" this approach asks, "Which of these scenarios for the future do you believe is most consistent with what you believe God is calling this congregation to be and to be doing?" An adaptation of that model is the theme of the last chapter. What can be done to jump-start a denomination that currently is immobilized by a dysfunctional system? Seven alternative scenarios constitute the case study that closes this book.

Every author is indebted to many other people for what goes into, or is left out of, a book. That is especially true with this book. Three-fourths of the first two drafts has been deleted. An incomplete list includes Bob Buford, John P. Casey, Carol Childress, Ruth Cleghorn, James H. Conner, B. Carlisle Driggers, Peter Drucker, Maxie Dunnam, Scott Field, Thomas Handy, James A. Harnish, Daniel A. Nielson, Barbara Oden, a computer named "Ornery," Agnes P. Schaller, Norman Shawchuck, W. Fred Smith, Glen J. Stewart, Jack Stubbs, J. V. Thomas, Dave Travis, William H. Willimon, and Charles Yrigoyen, Jr.

The only additional favor I ask of them is that they be forgiving of errors of fact and interpretation.

1.

Have You Felt the Earthquake?

An earthquake that registers at least 2.0 on the Richter scale strikes planet earth on the average of twice a day. Other earthquakes are shaking up the nation's economic and political systems.[1]

For at least three or four decades a huge earthquake has been shaking the foundations of Christianity all across the North American continent. What caused this earthquake?

A less than fully adequate explanation can be summarized in one word: competition. If a two-word explanation is acceptable, the second word is denial. The ecclesiastical marketplace is being shaken by an unprecedented degree of competition among the churches for new members. Relevance is replacing inherited institutional loyalties as a primary motivation when younger generations choose a church home. Quality is replacing geographical proximity. Credibility is replacing the power of kinship ties. A democratic "Made in America" model is replacing the imported European religious traditions. Large is replacing small as the descriptive term for where most people worship. New is replacing old. Trust is replacing distrust as the guiding principle in designing a denominational polity. Horizontal lines are now more powerful than vertical lines in institution building. Nondenominational is replacing denominational. Regional is replacing neighborhood in defining the service area of a parish.

One statistical indicator to measure the impact of this earthquake is to look at the distribution of congregations by denominational affiliation. Five of the categories in this table refer to current denominations and their predecessors while four are broad generic categories.

DISTRIBUTION OF CHRISTIAN CHURCHES (U.S.A.)

	1820	1906	1996
Southern Baptist Convention	N.A.	10%	13%
All Other Baptist Churches	*23%	16%	20%
United Methodist Church	24%	26%	12%
Roman Catholic Church	11%	6%	7%
Presbyterian (all)	14%	9%	5%
Lutheran (all)	7%	6%	7%
United Church of Christ	12%	7%	2%
Episcopal Church	5%	3%	3%
All others	4%	17%	31%

*The 1820 Baptist figure includes what later became the Southern Baptist Convention.

This table is based on the conservative estimate of 300,000 Christian congregations in the United States in 1996. The actual number, including house churches, may be closer to 350,000.

The earthquake-prone West Coast is where this redistribution of churches is most highly visible today and the number one example is Oregon followed by California. The category "All others" has grown far faster in those two states than it has back East where change moves at a slower pace. (For a statistical summary of a few of the changes in the American ecclesiastical landscape, see table I in the appendix.)

One of the most persuasive arguments for keeping denominational headquarters and the schools to train new generations of pastors east of the Mississippi River is that makes it easier to continue in a state of denial. "Earthquakes are a phenomenon of the West, they do not occur back here in the East. Therefore we can continue business as usual in our earthquake-proof headquarters back here."

A second expression of denial comes from those who believe their problems would disappear if only people were more committed. A third expression of denial comes in the pleas for churches to send more money to headquarters. A fourth is the proposal to restructure the denominational system around stronger vertical lines of authority.

Consequences and Victims

The consequences of this earthquake can be seen all across the ecclesiastical landscape. Perhaps the most significant long term implication is the shift in power and control from the professionals in the church to the laity. The critics describe this as putting the inmates in charge of running the insane asylum. The proponents applaud the response of the laity when they are challenged to be engaged in doing ministry rather than simply giving money and serving in meaningless committee assignments.

One example is congregational leadership. By 1970 most American denominations had adopted the European Roman Catholic model as the ideal. This called for every parish to be served by one or more seminary trained, full-time, and resident pastors. The number of Protestant seminaries has been greatly expanded and hundreds of millions of dollars have been contributed to finance this dream. The earthquake has toppled this model. A rapidly growing number of Roman Catholic parishes in the United States now have as their resident pastor a nun. At least 85,000, and perhaps as many as 100,000 Protestant churches are now served by a bivocational lay pastor or a bivocational team, and that number is growing by 2 percent annually.

Another victim of this earthquake, and a major theme of this book, is the old hierarchical denominational system built on vertical lines of authority. The severity of this earthquake has placed national denominational structures in a dozen of the largest Protestant denominations on the endangered species list. More and more congregations, who once looked up to their national denominational headquarters for direction, counsel, resources, and inspiration, are turning to other places for help. The successor often is a horizontal partnership with a parachurch organization and/or a teaching church and/or a commercial for-profit corporation (especially in the new Christian music, fund-raising, architectural services, and planning) and/or the independent publishing houses.

Another victim of this earthquake is the traditional approach to youth ministries. Throughout human history it was widely understood that a crucial role for adults was to socialize children and adolescents into the culture, values, and standards of behavior of that society. Youth looked up to adults for wisdom, guidance, knowledge, the lessons derived from years of experience, and counsel. One symbol of this pattern was that adults assigned to work with teenagers frequently carried the title "Youth Counselor."

The vast majority of the generation of teenagers born in the years 1970–82 failed to accept that model. It had been toppled by the earthquakes that were first felt in the 1960s that created the slogan, "Never trust anyone over thirty." Instead of turning to adults for wisdom, advice, and guidance, two-thirds of this generation of teenagers chose two other socializing forces—their peers and television.

Another victim of the earthquake was the old concept that called for the senior minister of the large congregation to fulfill the role as "head of staff." The new model calls for building a team of teams with many of the team members being lay volunteers.

For at least three decades before the earthquake, most new congregations in the United States were started by national and/or regional judicatories of three or four dozen denominations. That model was one of the first victims of the earthquake. The majority of new Christian congregations planted in North America this year will be started by congregations, independent entrepreneurial personalities, coalitions of congregations, parachurch organizations, and theological schools.

Perhaps the least widely discussed victim of the earthquake is the old assumption that each generation of churchgoers is theologically more liberal than the previous generation. That assumption toppled with the arrival of the generation of churchgoers born in the 1956–69 era. They are to be found in disproportionately large numbers in congregations that are theologically more conservative than that of their parents or older siblings.

Another victim is the old system of classifying categories of belief systems such as "fundamentalist," "liberal," and "conservative." The most useful postearthquake categories include terms such as the "postconservative evangelicals" and the "postliberals."[2]

Readers born before 1950 can recall the great and highly divisive battles fought in denominational circles in the 1920s, the 1950s, and especially the 1960s and 1970s, for the "soul" of the denomination, for control over theological schools, over the location of the denominational headquarters, over control of the decision-making processes of the denomination and its missional priorities, the use of quotas, denominational mergers, and the power to control the distribution of patronage. The deep chasm between congregational leaders and the national denominational leaders created by the earthquake has made those contests appear to be of less importance than who will be the president of the student body in the local high school.

Adults who have never seen it rain have difficulty understanding the severity of a drought. Likewise, none of the readers of this book can remember when vertical denominational lines were the norm and that design worked. One example of that occurred back in the 1917–1924 period when the Northern and Southern Methodists cooperated in the Centenary financial campaign. The theme celebrated the founding of the Methodist Missionary Society in 1819 and the end of the Great War in 1918. The funds were to be used for missions and European relief. A total of nearly $150 million was pledged in a top-down high pressure fund-raising drive. Thanks to the combination of the severe economic depression of the early 1920s and the high-pressure tactics, only $88 million was actually collected. Many were disappointed, several promises for missions could not be fulfilled, and a few called the whole effort a failure.

What really happened? How much was $88 million in 1922? First of all, that averaged out to approximately $16 per member in the two denominations.

Second, if those totals are translated into 1996 terms, the results are far more impressive. To purchase in 1996 what cost $88 million in 1922 requires $660 million. That $16 per member also was the equivalent of 3.6 percent of the average per capita personal income in 1922. Prepare for a shock—3.6 percent of the average per capita personal income in the United States in 1996 is $790. For The United Methodist Church, that would support a capital funds campaign of $6.8 billion in current dollars based on current levels of personal income!

Where are the national denominational leaders who today would recommend a national denominational capital funds campaign with a goal of raising even $500 for every member? The earthquake has destroyed those vertical lines of authority that made the Centenary Campaign an amazing success story.

Before the earthquake, the experts in several denominational publishing houses would design a new curriculum. After it was completed, representatives from the publishing houses would go out and introduce it to the staff of the various judicatories. Subsequently the regional staff introduced the new materials to congregational leaders and teachers.

The earthquake wiped out the foundations of that strategy. Today every published resource designed for congregational use must be prepared to earn and re-earn its place in an increasingly competitive marketplace. In reflecting on this, the president of one denominational publishing house explained, "We are going out of the curriculum business and into resourcing congregations."

For many classically trained church musicians the most disturbing consequence is that the earthquake destroyed much of the support for the traditional classical church music. Even worse, from their perspective, the reconstruction following the earthquake brought the new wave of contemporary Christian music that the most supportive and generous of these musicians describe as "trash." The good news is most of them soon will be able to retire.

One of the most far reaching consequences of the earthquake is a new operational definition of "church." Forty years ago "church" often was defined in terms of the denominational identity, the real estate, and a geographical definition of the area to be defined in terms of ministries and the people who are served.

One result of the earthquake is the emergence of the large regional church that is replacing the smaller neighborhood church. A second is the congregation with two or five or ten or twenty or a hundred different meeting places, each serving a relatively homogeneous slice of the population. This enables one congregation, with a relatively small paid staff and a huge number of volunteers, to serve people from a broad range of language, racial, ethnic, nationality, social, generational, economic, and educational backgrounds. On a typical weekend one-half of all worshipers may gather at one location and the other half be scattered among two or three dozen meeting places.[3]

Before the earthquake, the theologically more conservative churches often were organized around law and behavior. Today they are more likely to be organized around grace and salvation by faith.

Among the victims of this earthquake are the congregations that for decades depended largely on five sources of new members, (1) the children and grandchildren of their members, (2) newcomers to the community who were guided in the choice of a new church home by powerful denominational loyalties, (3) adults who married into that congregation, (4) Christians who preferred to walk to church, and (5) people who preferred the intimacy of the small church.

As was mentioned earlier, younger generations tend to choose a church home on the basis of (1) the relevance to their personal spiritual journey, (2) the quality of the ministry and (3) credibility. One result is huge competition for members born in the 1890–1920 era who reflect the old patterns.

In the early decades of the twentieth century, the number of American families who did not own a motor vehicle outnumbered those who did. After the earthquake, the number of American families owning three or more motor vehicles is larger than the number who do not own even one.

For some the most threatening consequence of this earthquake is the impact on traditional denominational structures. The easily measurable trend is the decreasing proportion of their total receipts that is being forwarded by congregations and regional judicatories to national denominational and ecumenical agencies. More significant is the sharp reductions in expectations that congregations and regional judicatories project of their churchwide agencies. Instead of turning to their national offices for help, both congregations and regional judicatories are looking to parachurch agencies, teaching churches, private consultants, faith-based and value-driven hospitals and for-profit corporations for the resources they seek.

One result is a growing demand for structural changes in the denominational systems. The Christian Church (Disciples of Christ) calls it "right sizing" as they contemplate reducing the number of general boards and enlarging their geographically defined regions. The United Church of Christ and the Southern Baptist Convention describe it as restructuring. The United Methodist Church is downsizing the system. Leaders in the ELCA are discussing the need for a new function and structure committee. The basic trend is to cut back on the national denominational structure and redesign the regional judicatories to enable them to (a) resource congregations more effectively and/or (b) concentrate on fulfilling the Great Commission.

Many of the older readers can remember the tremendous influence exerted by the National Council of Churches, one of the last great vertical structures in American Christianity, during the third quarter of the twentieth century. Its influence was felt by denominational, congregational, political, and educational leaders for many years. If one measures significance by the number of lives that have been transformed, however, a new horizontal partnership with congregations, called Promise Keepers, has had a far greater impact in five years than the National Council had in a quarter century.

For many older congregational leaders, the greatest shock from the earthquake has been the change in the role of the church council or vestry or session or consistory. Before the earthquake it was widely assumed that the primary role of the governing board was to serve as a permission-withholding body. The scarcity of resources that was a product of the Great Depression legitimatized that worldview. The 1950s, 1960s, and 1970s brought an era of abundance. That has enabled the governing board to transform its primary role from rationing scarce resources to designing a congregational strategy for a more competitive ecclesiastical marketplace—but that requires a new chapter.

2.

HAS YOUR CHURCH FELT THE EARTHQUAKE?

What will your congregation look like in the year 2021 or 2047? What will the next several decades bring to your church?

The one certain answer to that question, of course, is that only God knows. We also know that the earthquake in North American Christianity has changed the context for doing ministry. For many congregations this number one impact from the earthquake has been a sharp rise in the level of competition for future members. As recently as 1950, for example, the typical mainline Protestant congregation in the North was competing for new members with only one or two other churches of that same denomination plus two or three other mainline Protestant churches. In the South the Baptists competed against the Methodists, the Methodists competed with the Presbyterians, and the Presbyterians competed against the Episcopalians.

It Really Is Competitive!

Today most of the truly attractive Protestant congregations find their church shoppers already have visited two or three other congregations and have several others on their shopping list. The less attractive congregations are discovering they have relatively few church shoppers and 70 percent never return a second or third time. Many of these competing churches meet at a site ten to twenty miles from your building, perhaps one-third to one-half do not display a denominational label, several were founded within the past dozen years, one or two are led by a pastor reared in your denomination who left to become part of another tradition, and at least one owns a twenty acre or larger site at a highly visible location.

One consequence of this increased level of competition is a doubling of the population of a community may also be accompanied by a net loss in size in ten congregations, a net increase in size in seven others, and the founding of twenty new churches, three of which eventually become the largest Protestant congregations in that community.

To a substantial degree the future of your church will be determined by how effective you are in matching the competition in your ability to reach younger generations.

The Era of Rising Expectations

A second product of the earthquake is that younger adults of today project higher expectations than did their parents and grandparents. This is an issue being faced by retailers, the public schools, physicians, bankers, local governments, and automobile manufacturers.

Today's churchgoers expect far more from church than did their parents in the 1950s. They expect higher quality, more choices, greater relevance to their personal and spiritual needs, a vacant parking space at the end of the journey to church, and a variety of specialized ministries. Many also expect your congregation to be able to mobilize resources for ministries with people beyond your own membership.

The future of your congregation will be heavily influenced by how you respond to these rising expectations.

Is It Time to Relocate?

A third consequence of the earthquake is that during the next two decades at least 35,000 of today's American Protestant congregations will choose from among these three alternatives: (1) relocate to a new and better site and either buy or construct new physical facilities for a fresh start in a new era or (2) merge with another congregation or (3) cut back to a survival stance. At least 10 percent of today's congregations are meeting in obsolete facilities on inadequate sites at poor locations. What may have been a modern building on an adequate site at a good location in 1907 or 1927 or 1957 clearly is inadequate today.[1]

Who Will Choose Death?

Fourth, a reasonable guess is that 100,000 to 150,000 congregations will chose the easier route of dissolution during the next five decades. Many of those are congregations yet to be born, but the majority are now in existence. When confronted with the choice between change and dissolution, they will conclude it is easier to die. How many is 2,000 to 3,000 a year? That averages out to five to eight per day. During the past half century, an estimated eight congregations disappeared on the average day.

Who Will Be the Next Pastor?

Fifth, for many congregations the most influential variable in determing the health, vitality, size, role, and attractiveness of that church in 2046 lies in the identity of a pastor yet to be chosen. An excellent match between a gifted pastor with a twenty or thirty or forty year tenure and a good congregation will lead in one direction. Two or three serious mismatches will lead that congregation down a different road.

When Were You Born?

In addition to those five obvious factors, two other variables must be identified. One is the age of the congregation, or to be more precise, how long has this congregation been meeting in this building at this location?

If the answer is more than thirty-five years, the chances generally are at least three out of four that this is a congregation with an aging constituency that is either on a plateau in size or shrinking in numbers.

One of the big differences between the American ecclesiastical scene of 1906 and 1996 is the sharp increase in the number of congregations that have been in existence for at least fifty years. For example, in the Southern Baptist Convention, one-half of the congregations in existence in 1906 were less than twenty years old. In 1993, however, one-half were at least 65 years old. In The United Methodist Church, one-half of the 57,087 congregations in the six predecessor denominations in 1906 were less than twenty-five years old. Most of today's 36,500 United Methodist congregations trace their history back at least ninety years.

The numerically growing religious traditions report the majority of their congregations were founded since 1950. The most highly visible example is that rapidly growing number of independent churches.

How's Your Denomination's Health?

The second of these two widely neglected variables is the health and vitality of your whole denominational family. It is relatively easy to be a growing church in a denomination that is reaching younger generations and recent immigrants. It is much more difficult to be a numerically growing church in a denomination that is shrinking in size with an aging constituency.

The most obvious illustration of this is the source of new adult members. For example, in 1993 the parishes in the Evangelical Lutheran Church in America reported they received a combined total of 222,388 new confirmed members—and 85,000 or 38 percent were transfers from other Lutheran parishes.

In 1956 the two predecessor denominations of The United Methodist Church reported their churches received a total of nearly

320,000 members by intradenominational transfer or 46 percent of all new members received. In 1994 the churches of this denomination received a combined total of 131,000 members by intradenominational transfer, or 32 percent of all new members received.

In the numerically growing denomination that intradenominational flow of members is more likely to be greater than in the numerically shrinking religious tradition.

Who Cares?

All across American Protestantism there is a growing disinterest in what happens to national denominations. Who cares? Many congregational leaders and a growing number of pastors articulate feelings that can be summarized by words such as indifference, hostility, apathy, and disinterest.

This book has been written from the perspective of a denominationalist. I am convinced denominations are legitimate orders of God's creation. While my major concern and focus has been and is congregational life, I believe denominations can undergird the life, ministry, and outreach of the worshiping community. I also believe, with the apostle Paul, in the interdependence of the churches. I am intrigued by the growing interest among the leaders of independent or nondenominational churches to network with one another through such channels as the Willow Creek Association and the Leadership Network.

Why should you care about the future of your denomination? Among the reasons I would suggest are these:

(1) Self-interest. The healthier your denominational family, the more likely your congregation will be a healthy church. Ecclesiastical diseases often are contagious!

(2) The Great Commission. Far more important is the call to fulfill the Great Commission (Matthew 28:17-20). Partnerships between congregations and denominational agencies can be a highly effective way to fulfill the Great Commission.

(3) Interdependence. Denominational channels can be an effective means to enhance the degree of interdependence among the churches.

(4) Stewardship. Today's denominations represent a huge accumulation of resources including wisdom, expertise, loyalty, creativity, and money. It would be poor stewardship to write that off by passively watching their continued decline.

(5) Institutions. Literally thousands of valuable institutions are heavily dependent on the resources that denominational agencies are able to mobilize. These institutions include missionary posts, homes, camps, retreat centers, theological schools, colleges, and a huge variety of social welfare agencies.

(6) Congregational identity. While this has been undercut in recent years by denominational mergers, by the ecumenical movement, and by the erosion of institutional loyalties, tens of thousands of congregations continue to use their denominational affiliation as a central component of their identity. This is especially strong within the Lutheran Church-Missouri Synod, the Southern Baptist Convention, the Seventh-day Adventist Church, the Roman Catholic Church, and several dozen other religious traditions.

A useful replacement for that is to build a congregation's local identity around its own distinctive ministry, but that is easier said than done.

What would you add to that list of reasons for perpetuating and renewing denominational systems?

For a different perspective on this question about the role of denominations, it may be useful to look first at the reflections of leaders of independent churches and, second, at the experiences of two other denominational systems.

3.

Can We Learn from the Competition?

Anyone responsible for designing either a denominational or a congregational strategy should recognize three facts of life. First, that congregation—or denomination—does not exist all by itself out there on the ecclesiastical playing field.

Second, as has been emphasized repeatedly earlier, the level of competition on that playing field is much higher today than it was forty or seventy years earlier. What earned a church a grade of A- on its ministry in 1956 produces a grade of C or C+ in 1996.

Third, it is possible to learn from the competition. In his autobiography, Sam Walton, the founder of the Walmart chain of discount stores, explained that whenever he had the opportunity, he would walk through a KMart store. In the 1970s and early 1980s, KMart was Walton's number one competitor. It is not uncommon today, for example, for the senior minister of the second largest Protestant church in town to take a Sunday morning off and go worship with the largest Protestant congregation in that community. Likewise, many pastors spend part of their vacation visiting a congregation that resembles the church they serve or resembles the church they hope their congregation will become in the years ahead.

As recently as the 1950s, most churchgoers picked a congregation on the basis of one or more of these six criteria: (1) kinship ties, (2) nationality, language, or racial heritage, (3) inherited denominational loyalties, (4) geographical convenience, (5) what that church offered their children, or (6) the doctrinal stance of that church.

The generations born after 1955 are more likely to choose a church home on the basis of these three criteria: (1) relevance to one's personal and spiritual journey, (2) the quality of all aspects of the ministry from an abundance of convenient off-street parking to the quality of communication of the preacher, and (3) credibility—does this congregation live out what it proclaims?

One result is an unprecedented migration of church members from one congregation to another. Another is an unprecedented high level of competition among congregations for future members. A heavily traveled road in this increasingly competitive ecclesiastical world is the migration of younger adults from denominationally affiliated congregations to independent churches. Why is this happening?

What Do the Independents Say?

When the pastors of these independent churches are asked to identify the advantages they enjoy when compared to one of the denominationally-affiliated churches, these eight are heard frequently.

(1) Our focus on ministry and missions is never diverted by a pronouncement or a decision from denominational headquarters that may anger many of our members.

(2) Since no one comes here because of inherited denominational loyalties, we must earn and re-earn the continued loyalty of every one of our members and of new generations.

(3) We are free to create our own traditions. The creativity of our people is not restricted because of a need to conform to someone else's definition of the appropriate institutional traditions. The five most highly visible examples of this are in governance, real estate,

music, worship, and community outreach. We do not have to secure approval from other churches on where we can locate our meeting place, we are free to focus on a participatory approach to worship, we are free to utilize contemporary Christian music, we are free to launch a variety of off-campus ministries, we can custom design our system of governance to fit our unique role, and we can create our own channels of community outreach rather than feel guilty about not supporting community ministries created by earlier generations in other churches.

(4) We enjoy the challenges and the responsibilities that go with being completely self-expressing, self-governing, self-financing, and self-propagating. We are not diverted by the regulatory role of a denominational system[1] nor weakened by denominational subsidies.

(5) We design our own criteria for evaluating candidates for positions on the paid staff. Thus we are able to (a) give a high priority to character, the clarity of that person's call from God to ministry, Christian commitment, competence, enthusiasm, productivity, and specialized skills, (b) place a comparatively low value on academic and denominational credentials, and (c) draw many or most of our paid staff out of our own membership—and thus gain the advantage of staff who fully understand and are supportive of the unique culture of this congregation.

We also have to be prepared to carry the full responsibility for terminating the relationship with an unwanted or unneeded staff member when that day does come. We learn to live with the future consequence of current decisions.

(6) We are not limited to the resources created by any one denominational system. We can pick and choose and customize the resources we need from that rapidly growing array of suppliers, including denominational agencies.

(7) By definition as an independent church, we are forced to trust our own volunteer leaders. We have nowhere else to turn. Next to God's goodness, that may be our greatest strength.

(8) We can design our own local outreach ministries and choose the worldwide ministries we want to support on the basis of our

own criteria. That makes it easier to mobilize resources for both sets of needs.

Many of these pastors, most of whom were reared in a denominational church, are quick to add there are disadvantages to being in an independent congregation. That list often includes (1) the absence of any system to protect the pastor when a group of members want that pastor to leave, (2) the absence of a denominational fellowship (in recent years a number of parachurch organizations have moved to fill that vacuum), (3) the lack of access to low interest loans and grants for construction of new facilities, (4) the absence of a well-run denominational pension and health insurance program, (5) the absence of a sense of interdependence with other churches (that vacuum is being filled by a variety of parachuch organizations and movements), (6) the absence of an automatic flow of new members who are attracted by the denominational label, and (7) the absence of a sense of identity and cohesion that can be reinforced with a denominational affiliation.

Those reflections may be useful to anyone who wants to design a new denominational structure that combines the best of two worlds—the advantages that go with a denominational affiliation and the advantages enjoyed by the independent or nondenominational churches.

What Did Texas Baptists Do?

If one is open to learning from other denominations, a useful lesson can be learned from the largest state convention in the Southern Baptist Convention. For nearly twenty years the Baptist General Convention of Texas has been vulnerable to several internal battles. One was the denomination-wide quarrel between the fundamentalists and the conservatives that began over control of the national denominational agencies and seminaries, but eventually was reflected within the various state conventions. A second was the decision by Baylor University to sever its institutional ties to the denomination. A third was the sudden dismissal of the popular president of Southwestern Baptist Theological Seminary.

Any one of these could have blossomed into a bitter and divisive battle.

What happened? The Southern Baptists of Texas were challenged to plant 1,400 new missions over the next four years. Instead of choosing up sides, the top priority was given to a unifying missional challenge.

Is it wiser to focus on the issues that divide? Or the causes that unite?

Who Reaches the Post-1955 Generations?

A different perspective suggests other lessons that can be learned from the competition. What are the qualities and characteristics of the congregations, whether denominationally related or independent, that are reaching large numbers of the generations born after 1955?

That question is far too complex for a single factor analysis. It is safe to suggest, however, that most of these competitors, and many do carry a denominational affiliation, display at least a dozen of these characteristics.

(1) They project comparatively high expectations of people and the worship attendance-to-membership ratio is above 70 percent.

(2) The sermons focus on the what and the why, not the how.[2] Instead of addressing the question of how to be a better Christian or how to support a denominational goal, the preacher is more likely to focus on what it means to be a Christian or why Christians do not conform to worldly patterns or what is required to enrich one's spiritual journey or what it means to accept Jesus Christ as Lord and Savior or what Christians believe.

(3) More attention in designing a ministry plan is given to the hurts, the needs, and the spiritual journey of the people than to the traditions of that congregation or the preferences of the staff.

(4) While evangelism continues to be a high priority, by year seven of that congregation's history, more resources are allocated to transforming believers into disciples and challenging and training disciples to be engaged in doing ministry than are devoted to

persuading nonbelievers to become believers. The transformation of lives is a higher priority than expanding the knowledge base of the people.

(5) Typically these churches enjoy pastorates of fifteen to fifty years.[3] This reflects the fact that today people prefer to focus on relationships rather than roles. When John Wesley wrote in 1756 that a year was too long for a preacher to serve one pastoral charge, he was reflecting an era when the role of the preacher was perceived to be far more important than the relationships a pastor enjoyed. It is not irrelevant to note that in recent years an increasing number of the laity refer to their minister as "Pastor" rather than as "Preacher." Relationships are replacing role!

(6) The women's ministries focus heavily on relationships, rather than on events or programs, and usually include a variety of mutual support groups with a strong emphasis on healing.

(7) Prayer and the prayer life of the people is a very high priority in the allocation of scarce resources.

(8) A high priority is given to learning opportunities for adults.

(9) The group life is vital, healthy, and expanding and includes many men's groups.

(10) The hymns, the sermons, and the prayers are more likely to exalt the second or third person of the Trinity rather than the first.[4]

(11) The pastor or senior minister displays many of the gifts and skills of the effective entrepreneur.

(12) The congregation either (a) was founded after 1960 or (b) relocated to the present meeting place after 1960.

(13) The congregation owns an adequate supply of off-street parking and this enables it to draw and serve people from a ten to twenty mile radius. The leaders accept and affirm the role as a regional, rather than as a neighborhood church.

(14) It is located on the evangelical two-thirds of the theological spectrum.

(15) The value of high quality is fully accepted and that becomes a driving force in planning and in doing ministry.

(16) The congregation averages more than two hundred at worship. (See table VII in the appendix.)

(17) The worship service is a relatively fast-paced experience.

(18) The seven-day-a-week program offers a variety of meaningful choices to people in worshiping, learning, serving, and caring.

(19) A comprehensive training program provides relevant training for all volunteers. The staff see themselves primarily as trainers rather than as doers.

(20) At least one nontraditional worship experience with contemporary Christian music is offered every week. A common pattern is one traditional worship service, one nontraditional, and one that is identified as "blended." A small but growing number of congregations offer concurrent services—one traditional and one nontraditional—early Sunday morning and another pair of concurrent, but different worship experiences at the late hour.

(21) In the large multiple staff congregations, the paid staff include relatively few full-time ordained generalists and many part-time or full-time lay specialists. Frequently the staff is organized around the concept of a team of teams rather than as a federation of individual and isolated empires.

(22) The driving force in program planning is the identification of the personal and spiritual needs of people rather than on what that congregation always has offered.

(23) The ministry is especially attractive to parents with very young children.

(24) A higher priority is given to challenging the laity to be engaged in doing ministry off campus than is given to raising and sending money away to hire other people to be engaged in missional ventures.

While that is far from an exhaustive list, it does illustrate two points. First, it is a highly competitive ecclesiastical environment for future church members. Second, the reflections of the pastors of independent churches and the characteristics of the congregations that are reaching younger generations should be of interest to anyone designing new wineskins for your congregation or your denomination to use in the twenty-first century.

Who Reaches the New Immigrants?

What are the two crucial variables that will determine the future of your denomination? The historical record is clear. The numerically growing denominations are those that are most effective in reaching, attracting, serving, and assimilating (1) younger generations of American-born residents of the United States and (2) recent immigrants to these shores.

From the post–Civil War era through the 1920s, the most widely used strategy was designed around starting new congregations to reach younger generations and planting new missions to serve the recent immigrants. During the 1880s, for example, more than 9,000 new Methodist congregations were organized that were still in existence in 1906. Nearly 2,200 of these were organized by the three large Negro Methodist denominations of that day. During the 1880–1899 years, nearly 5,000 Lutheran parishes were organized, an average of twenty per month. The Northern Baptists planted an average of ten new churches a month during the 1880s and 1890s while the Southern Baptists were starting an average of thirty a month, the National Baptist Convention (Colored) was starting an average of nearly forty a month, the Congregationalists were starting an average of eight every month, and the Roman Catholic Church was organizing an average of sixteen new parishes every month.

In recent years, five different strategies have been followed by various denominations in their efforts to reach younger generations and recent immigrants.

The strategy most widely used, the most difficult, and one with limited success has been to encourage long-established congregations to invite and assimilate all varieties of unchurched people.

A second, a highly effective and creative strategy has been to challenge congregations to launch off-campus ministries to reach people who would never come to the intimidating meeting place of that missionary-minded church. One off-campus ministry may be with recent immigrants from Cambodia, a second with upper-middle-class Anglo young never-married adults, a third with residents of a mobile home park, a fourth with single parent mothers, a fifth with recent newcomers from Mexico, a sixth with undergraduates at the local community college, a seventh with recent immigrants from Brazil, an eighth with one segment of the black population, a ninth with residents of a retirement community, and a tenth with young families moving into a new residential community.

In each of these off-campus worshiping communities, the ultimate goal is to create a self-expressing, self-governing, self-financing, and self-propagating Christian congregation with indigenous leadership.

A third strategy has been to encourage existing congregations and coalitions of churches to plant new missions rather than simply send money to denominational headquarters. In those denominations where the polity permits it, this has been highly effective.

A fourth strategy has been based on the assumption that the best beginning point for a denomination in which at least 90 percent of the constituency comes from a white European ancestry, is to place persons from an ethnic or racial minority ancestry in highly visible positions. This will "prove" to everyone that the denomination is eager to welcome people from an ethnic or racial minority background.

The most effective strategy, however, has been a return to the late-nineteenth-century model and is illustrated by one middle-sized denomination.

What Did the Alliance Do?

The Christian and Missionary Alliance traces its origins back to a Presbyterian minister, Dr. A. B. Simpson, who launched the movement in 1881. It has been organized around two focal points, (1) the exaltation of the second person of the Holy Trinity and (2) missionary endeavors. By 1968 it had grown to include 72,000 members scattered among 1,128 congregations in North America.

In the mid-1970s the denominational leaders challenged the congregations to do what everyone knew was impossible—to start new missions to reach new immigrants and new generations. Between 1975 and 1994 this middle-sized denomination increased the number of ethnic and racial minority congregations from 105 to 512 including 73 Hmong congregations, 76 Spanish language churches, 61 Chinese congregations, 53 Korean, 58 Vietnamese, and 46 Cambodian. In 1994 this denomination included 148,000 members or 305,000 adherents scattered among 1,958 congregations in the United States.

The United Methodist Church included 58 times as many members in 1994 and reported 17 times as many baptisms as the Alliance.

How did the Christian and Missionary Alliance, after decades of very slow growth, become a model of a multicultural denomination?

Why has the Alliance been so effective in reaching recent immigrants and younger generations? That is a far more complex question than it first appears and includes several variables. One reason, of course, can be found in their name. This is a missionary church! But Methodism began in America as a missionary movement. Evangelism and missions were at the heart of American Methodism for more than a hundred and fifty years.

A second factor is that the Alliance projects high expectations of people, but American Methodism was founded as a high expectation religious movement. Compare the lifestyle of the Alliance pastor of 1996 with the Methodist circuit rider of 1796, and today's Alliance pastor lives in what can be described, in relative terms, as somewhere between extravagance and opulence.

A third variable is that the Christian and Missionary Alliance is organized to enable leaders to lead, to foster innovation, and to support creativity. To use Robert Putnam's term, the Alliance is rich in social capital.[5] It is organized around a combination of a clearly defined theological position and a central focus on Jesus Christ as Savior, Sanctifier, Healer, and Lord; a high level of trust of local leadership; cohesive networks, and high expectations; a rich history of effective missionary work on other continents and especially in Asia; a continuing passion for evangelism and missions; and the assumption that denominational leaders can and should lead. That cultural context not only enabled the leaders to challenge congregational leaders, it also produced a remarkable response!

It also should be noted that the Christian and Missionary Alliance has displayed a high degree of organizational flexibility. For administrative purposes the Alliance is divided into 33 districts in the United States. One-third of those are geographically defined districts and the other 11 are nongeographical intercultural districts.

In addition, the Alternative Education Program, begun in 1976, was designed to train Native Americans "to extend any person, wherever he lives or whatever his schedule, the opportunity to follow the call of God and be trained for ministry."

If the goal is to reach recent immigrants to the United States and to become a multicultural denomination, useful lessons can be learned from the Christian and Missionary Alliance.

4.

WHAT'S AHEAD FOR YOUR DENOMINATION?

One of the great essays on leadership uses the metaphor of the wagon master who led the wagon trains across the great plains and mountains to the Pacific Coast in the latter part of the nineteenth century. The author, J. S. Ninomiya, declares the wagon master had two crucial responsibilities. The first was to get up in the morning, point to the west, and declare, "Folks, that's the direction we're going today." The second was to maintain a reasonable level of peace, harmony, cooperation, and teamwork among the members of the wagon train and to keep petty grievances from becoming disruptive diversions.[1]

It cannot be emphasized too strongly that everyday the wagon master pointed west—to what for that party was new, unexplored, and often threatening territory. The wagon master did not recommend returning east.

Do You Have a Wagon Master?

This raises two questions that apply to both congregations and to denominational systems. First, do you have a wagon master? Who is pointing the direction you should travel? The pastor? The governing board? An ad hoc long-range planning committee? The president of your denomination? The executive committee? The chief executive officer of your regional judicatory? A special task force on preparing to do ministry in the twenty-first century?

Several denominations, such as the Evangelical Lutheran Church in America (ELCA), the Christian and Missionary Alliance, and the Evangelical Free Church are structured to provide the position of full-time wagon master. Others, like the Southern Baptist Convention, have a part-time position for a temporary national wagon master, but they elect a new one every year or two. That means the full-time chief executive for each of the state conventions can assume the role of wagon master for that region.

Likewise the synod bishop in the ELCA can serve as the wagon master for that synod by earning the respect and trust required for that role. Various regions in the Christian Church (Disciples of Christ) have enjoyed the leadership of a long-tenured wagon master.

The regulatory polity of the Presbyterian Church (U.S.A.) makes it more difficult for the Stated Clerk of the denomination or for presbytery executives to assume the role of wagon master.

The polity of The United Methodist Church, which is organized around distrust of individuals, makes it impossible for anyone to serve as the wagon master. The closest to a wagon master in that denomination is the Conference Board of Ordained Ministry, which chooses the future generations of parish pastors.

A common alternative in both congregational and denominational circles is to leave that position vacant and encourage the members of that wagon party either to (a) choose their own direction and pace or (b) spend the day quarreling over the direction to be followed.

Which Direction?

The second critical issue is the direction to go. Should we go back to the familiar surroundings of the East? Or continue to move toward a new tomorrow?

In both congregational and denominational circles the direction that is most likely to win broad support is to seek to return to a highly romanticized version of 1955. In the Christian and Missionary Alliance, as was described earlier, the decision was to move from a largely Anglo constituency to become a multicultural religious tradition. Currently the direction chosen in the Southern Baptist Convention is to (a) change from a Southern and Southwestern constituency into a national denomination and (b) reach new generations and recent immigrants by planting thousands of new missions before the end of this millennium. In other traditions, the decision has been to appoint a committee to serve as the wagon master and define the direction.

This issue of direction is far more complicated than it first appears because a long journey brings many forks in the road. One, of course, is do we even want a wagon master to lead us? Another was raised earlier and merits elaboration.

Vertical or Horizontal?

Why do units of local government in northern Italy excel when compared to units of local government in southern Italy? In a remarkable analysis of the local governments of Italy, Robert D. Putnam and his colleagues concluded that the key variable was in their social and political culture. For nearly a millennium southern Italy had been organized in a rigidly hierarchical system with a heavy emphasis on "vertical bonds." By contrast, the social and political culture of northern Italy had been organized around "horizontal bonds." The small organizations in the North resembled voluntary associations built on the trust of people for one another.[2]

Should the new design for the denomination be one that emphasizes horizontal lines? Or should the emphasis be on strengthening the vertical lines? One example of horizontal lines is the partnership between two or three or four congregations and the regional judicatory in planting a new mission. A second is the mentoring church that works with two or three other congregations in helping them design and implement a strategy for a new day. A third is the coalition between two or three church owned and operated nursery schools, the local elementary school, and the parents in preparing three-and four-year-old children for the day when they enter kindergarten. A fourth is the partnership between a national agency, a dozen self-identified teaching churches, and one or two theological schools in creating a national network of teaching churches.

Systems built on vertical lines naturally tend to urge, "Send us money and people so we can do what you cannot do." That naturally creates the self-fulfilling prophecy that denominational systems are needed to do what congregations and regional judicatories do not know how to do or cannot be trusted to do and that raises another question about trust.

Institutions or People?

Every society chooses between two paths. One is to trust people. The other is to trust those institutions the people have created.[3] From 1880 up through the 1940s, with an occasional exception, the American culture was organized around the assumption that social, political, labor, educational, and religious institutions could be trusted. This provided a compatible cultural environment for religious bodies, such as the United Presbyterian Church, the Episcopal Church, the Christian Reformed Church, the Roman Catholic Church, The Methodist Church, and a few other denominations that were organized on the principle that while sinful human beings cannot be trusted, institutions can and should be trusted.

The Civil Rights Movement of the 1950s emerged to challenge that assumption. Many more challenges were issued by the generation born in the 1942–55 era. The opposition to the war in Vietnam, the disruption at the 1968 national convention of the Democratic Party, Watergate, the rise of investigative reporting, and a variety of public scandals undermined the public's trust in institutions. The pendulum has swung.

In commenting on this, the eminent philosopher John R. Searle has written, "One of the most fascinating—and terrifying—features of the era in which I write this is the steady erosion of acceptance of large institutional structures round the world."[4]

The Protestant Reformation also was about trust. It had become clear to many reformers that the Roman Catholic Church was a corrupt institution. It no longer could be trusted. The most conservative of the reformers apparently concluded the problem was not in the institution, but rather in the sinful people who had corrupted a holy institution. Over a period of nearly three centuries, Ignatius of Loyola, founder of the Jesuits in 1534, and other Catholic reformers raised the moral tone and brought a new spiritual vitality to that branch of Christianity.

Another relatively conservative group of reformers included Martin Luther, John Calvin, and (later) John Wesley who began to distrust both old institutions and the people who staffed them. Their solution was to create new institutions that could be the recipients of the people's trust if they were carefully regulated by new generations of trustworthy people.

The revolutionaries of that era were the Anabaptists. They did not trust institutions to speak for God. They also distrusted the natural urges of sinful human beings. They called people to live by a very high moral code and for many, the New Testament was the only unreserved recipient of their trust.

As we close out the second millennium, this same question is facing the people who have been given the responsibility for restructuring their denominational system.

Who can be trusted? In the 1950s, the cultural environment in the United States made it easy for adults born before 1935 to reply, "Scripture, the denominational system, and the people whom God has called to staff that system."

Forty years later, younger adults are more likely to respond to that question, "The leading of the Holy Spirit, Jesus Christ, Scripture, me, and those individuals who have earned my trust."

In an influential book, Francis Fukuyama describes trust as "social capital" that is an increasingly valuable asset in an increasingly competitive world.[5] He also declares that trust is an essential component of a strategy for building voluntary associations. Trust also is social capital that could help resource the transformation of several denominations.

The question today is which individuals and institutions can be trusted? One answer is those who are prepared to earn and to re-earn the trust of the people. A second answer is people we have learned to trust, but not institutions staffed by strangers. That provides a big advantage to the staff of the regional judicatory and to the officials in the small denomination where that official or staff person can be personally acquainted with several people in every congregation. This reduces the distrust of institutions and places the staff in the very large and anonymous churchwide agencies in the large denominations at a tremendous disadvantage. (A parallel pattern can be seen in labor unions, the United States Congress, and partisan politics.)

One response to this swing of the pendulum is to redesign the system to affirm the conviction that people can be trusted. As was mentioned earlier, that swing led to the use of primary elections to nominate candidates for the presidency, rather than leaving those decisions to the national conventions of each political party.

A second alternative is to look for a bigger hammer to enforce that growing list of regulations. A third is to attempt to halt the swing of the pendulum and push it in the other direction. A fourth is simply to go out of business. A fifth is to appoint a committee. A sixth is to study the life expectancy tables to determine whether the people born in the old era of trusting institutions will outlive the younger people who were born into a world that taught them to distrust institutions and trust only those individuals who earn one's trust.

Distrust is a central characteristic of most of the European religious traditions. That is one of several reasons to explain the inability of the mainstream Protestant denominations to reach third and fourth generation American-born churchgoers. Should your denomination plan to enter the twenty-first century with a polity reflecting the European religious culture of distrust of the laity? Or should it design a new system built on trust?

Within The United Methodist Church the level of internal distrust is far higher today than it was in the early decades of the nineteenth century. The uneducated circuit rider was the recipient of a higher level of trust than is today's seminary graduate with nineteen or twenty years of formal education. A significant increase in the distrust of the laity began to surface in the pre–Civil War era when an increasing number of Methodist circuit riders were assigned to stations. Those occasional visits from the circuit rider had placed heavy responsibilities in the class leaders, the local preacher, and the exhorter. The full-time presence on the local scene of the resident pastor reduced the need to trust lay leadership.[6]

After the Civil War, the lay-created and lay-run organizations, such as the Sunday School Union and the Tract Society, that had been organized a couple of generations earlier, were placed under the control of the General Conference. The next step was to place clergymen in charge of these bureaucratic organizations.[7]

More recently the requirement of a seminary degree for ordination meant that the socialization process for the future ministers should be entrusted to professional educators, not to the members of congregations nor to pastors of larger congregations.

In 1906 the Methodist Episcopal Church trusted immigrants from Europe, many with limited formal education, to administer their own monocultural nongeographical annual conferences. Ninety years later, when recent immigrants from Asia, many with high levels of formal education, requested that they be trusted to create and administer their own monocultural and nongeographic annual conferences, the response of the 1996 General Conference was that issue required additional study.

At this point in this discussion of trust, the baseball fans may enjoy a brief analogy.

What Happened to Major League Baseball?

The signing of the National Agreement in 1903 brought peace between the old National League and the new American League. That agreement included the reserve clause that bound a player to the club that originally signed him. For the next sixteen years major league baseball earned the trust of millions of fans. Then in 1919 the Black Sox betting scandal undermined that trust. Judge Kene-saw Mountain Landis was chosen by the owners in 1921 to be the first commissioner. He was granted unlimited authority to act in the best interests of the game. Judge Landis restored the public's trust in the institution.

Major league baseball was owned and operated by white males with European ancestors. The cultural environment of that era supported the assumption that the owners, the commissioner, and the system could be trusted. They knew better than the fans or the players what would be good for the game. They designed the contracts, determined the salaries to be paid, set the price of tickets, and ran the game. A few fans complained when the Browns left St. Louis, the Dodgers left Brooklyn, the Athletics left Philadelphia, the Giants left New York, the Braves left Boston, and the Senators left Washington, but the game was in good hands. The owners, the commissioner, and the system could be trusted!

It was not a coincidence that the first player to go to court to challenge the assumption that the team owned the players and could trade them without the player's permission was a black man. Curt Flood filed that suit in late 1969. He lost. In the summer of 1972 the United States Supreme Court rejected his appeal.[8]

Flood lost that battle, but the players won the war. The old system no longer controls the game. When asked whom they trust, today's players tend to respond, "Me, my agent, and my attorney."

Who were the players to lead that revolution against the old institution? It is worth noting the birth years of the leading revolu-tionaries—Andy Messersmith (1945), Dave McNally (1942), Ted Simmons (1949), Jim Hunter (1946), Bill Lee (1946), John Bench (1947), Reggie Jackson (1946), and Curt Flood (1938).

The baseball owners had to make a decision in the early 1970s. They could hope fans would pay to come out to see a fifty-year-old white center fielder, a sixty-year-old baserunner, and a fifty-five-year-old pitcher. Or they could grant the younger players the right of free agency, which came in 1976.

That generation born in the early and mid-1940s not only revo-lutionized professional baseball, they also revolutionized labor unions, the universities, partisan politics, banking, television, journalism—and the churches.

This also left the mainline Protestant denominations with two choices. Should we hope the generations born before 1940, who believe in trusting institutions, will live forever? Or should we change the system to enable us to reach younger generations?

Medieval or American?

One of the critical forks in the road for all Christian traditions in North America reflects the growing gap between those that reflect a strong medieval European cultural and religious heritage and those that reflect a "Made in America" democratic and religious culture.

The most highly visible examples in the United States of a religious culture reflecting the medieval European world are the Roman Catholic Church and The United Methodist Church. Both are organized on the assumptions that institutions can be trusted, but the people, especially the laity and congregational leaders, cannot be trusted. Both have experienced close to a 25 percent decrease in worship attendance since 1960. Both have experienced an exodus of people born after 1955 who were reared in that religious tradition.

Both reflect the medieval European culture that flourished in the closing centuries of the first millennium and the first centuries of the second millennium. It was designed to produce security and safety. The price tag on those goals was dependency.[9] The central dynamic of feudalism was a simple exchange system. In the earliest stages, a Frankish (German) band of warriors gave their allegiance and skills to the chieftain of the *comitatus* in exchange for a share of the loot. Later small landowners, freemen, and warriors (vassals) gave their allegiance, their service, and even their possessions to an overlord in exchange for protection. Governance was based on the whim of the ruler, not the rule of law.[10] The medieval feudal system was built on a high level of control by the overlords, but that was matched by the obligations owed the vassals and the peasants. In a natural, normal, and predictable sequence, the overlords gradually sought to expand their control. When that was not matched by an increase in the rewards and obligations to the underlords, they revolted.

It is worth noting that in England the feudal system eventually was challenged by the barons on the grounds of excessive taxation—King Richard I demanded that more and more money be sent to headquarters. A second motivation was the arbitrary rule of the king. It also is worth noting that the first effort at reform in 1213 failed. It was not until 1215, at Runnymede, that King John reluctantly agreed to the terms of the Magna Carta. That was the beginning of the end of feudalism in England, but three revisions of that great charter were issued during the next decade. The first effort at reform often fails. The second and third usually require subsequent revisions and improvements.

The concept of the episcopacy was compatible with that feudal culture. In northern Europe a bishop was expected to fill both the role of a spiritual ruler and a secular lord. The bishop owed allegiance to a secular overlord. The bishop was expected to preside over a court of canon law, to be accountable for the behavior of the clergy in that diocese, to discover and root out heresy, and to identify those who eventually would be elevated to sainthood. The bishop was a logical, natural, and compatible component of a vast hierarchical system. Eventually, however, a competitive system of commerce undermined and destroyed that feudal culture in Europe.

The contemporary American Methodist and Roman Catholic version of the European feudal system calls for a minister to be guaranteed an appointment at or above minimum compensation in exchange for an agreement to go where sent by the bishop. Allegiance is exchanged for security. A congregation is guaranteed (a) a local monopoly on the denominational franchise in that neighborhood, (b) a pastor, and (c) a connectional tie in exchange for allegiance, a surrender of local control, and money to be sent to the conference.

This observer is convinced that this model of a religious culture based on a European feudal culture is incompatible with the democratic values of contemporary American society.

The current American version of that medieval heritage was designed on the assumption that while people cannot be trusted, institutions and superior officials can be trusted. John Wesley expressed that distrust by keeping title to Methodist chapels in his name until shortly before his death. One United Methodist version of that distrust is the reversionary clause in the title to property and the requirement that congregationally initiated proposals on real estate must be approved by a district committee. A second expression of the many examples of distrust is in ministerial placement. Neither the pastors nor the parishioners can be trusted to make wise decisions.

When they approach this fork in the road to the twenty-first century, younger generations and recent immigrants are choosing the churches located on the path labeled "Made in America." These include nearly all black and African American congregations, most independent congregations, plus such denominations as the Assemblies of God, the Church of the Nazarene, the Seventh-day Adventist Church, the Southern Baptist Convention, the Church of Jesus Christ of Latter-day Saints, the Reorganized Church of Jesus Christ of Latter-day Saints, several expressions of the Church of God, a variety of Bible churches, and several Pentecostal traditions. The Evangelical Free Church in America may be the best example of a denomination with European roots that has become almost completely Americanized.[11]

The heavily traveled path by younger generations at this fork in the road is labeled "Made in America." The lightly traveled path is labeled "Made in Europe." Korean Christians are among the few immigrant congregations that reflect a "both-and" response—thanks largely to Presbyterian and Methodist missionaries who went to Korea in the last quarter of the nineteenth century.

Distrust or Challenge?

From this observer's perspective one of the two most crucial forks in the road in designing a new denominational structure reflects this European-American context. The European traditions, especially Roman Catholic, Methodist, and to a lesser extent, Presbyterian, are built on the assumption that the laity in general and congregational leaders in particular cannot be trusted.

Younger generations and new immigrants tend not to be attracted to any institution that is organized on the principle that people cannot be trusted.

While this observer is convinced the Southern Baptist Convention resembles a "Made in America" religious tradition, the battles in recent years over control of Baptist institutions suggest that several of the contemporary national leaders were born in central Europe in the seventeenth or eighteenth centuries while others were reared Presbyterian or Methodist.

By contrast, the earlier internal quarrels over control of institutions in the Lutheran Church-Missouri Synod, which also is organized around a strong emphasis on congregational autonomy, were a normal, natural, and predictable consequence of the Americanization of a Germanic religious heritage. Similar struggles over control versus trust have emerged in recent years in several other European heritage traditions including the Christian Reformed Church, the Episcopal Church, the Presbyterian Church (U.S.A.), the Reformed Church in America, and the Evangelical Lutheran Church in America as well as in both the Republican and Democratic parties. The notable recent political expression of control versus trust has been the shift from nominating candidates for the presidency in national political conventions to reliance on state primary elections.

Examples of systemic distrust in The United Methodist Church include these assumptions: (1) any full ministerial member of the annual conference is qualified to serve any appointment that the cabinet chooses for that person; (2) the cabinet is more competent than congregational leaders to choose the best qualified available pastor for a particular congregation; (3) the denomination is better equipped than any candidate for the ministry to determine the training a candidate will need to be an effective pastor (while no one can prove a cause-and-effect relationship, the numerical decline in both predecessor denominations coincided with the requirement of both a college and a seminary degree for ordination); (4) the ministerial marketplace will function most effectively on a small regional (conference or episcopal area) basis rather than as a national marketplace; (5) ministers cannot be trusted to choose where they can serve most effectively; (6) the most effective system for "doing missions" is for congregations to send money and a few personnel to the denomination who will "do missions" rather than to trust and challenge the laity to be engaged in missional outreach; (7) the laity cannot be trusted to choose the final destination for their benevolence dollars; (8) people should and will choose a church home on the basis of geographical proximity and/or inherited denominational loyalties; (9) younger generations of Americans should and will be comfortable with that European hierarchical feudal culture; (10) congregational leaders no longer can be trusted, as they were as recently as the 1920s, on when and where to plant new missions; (11) congregational leaders cannot be trusted to decide unilaterally on the appropriate location of their meeting place nor on the design for the construction of new facilities; (12) church members cannot be trusted to determine their own response to a lengthening series of political, economic, and social policy questions such as divorce, the military draft, immigration, American foreign policy, abortion, human sexuality, the federal budget, and farm policy and need the advice of denominational officials in order to understand the Christian position on these issues; (13) the wisest allocation of scarce financial resources can be made by people high in that hierarchical system and the donors cannot be trusted to make those decisions; (14) institutional, vocational, and economic dependency is a healthy condition and should be encouraged; (15) upward dependency is a useful means of assuring accountability; (16) the most useful yardsticks for evaluating congregational life (and ministerial effectiveness) are (a) the unquestioned loyalty and support of denominational decisions and goals, and (b) the amount of money sent to conference headquarters; and (17) the people in the pews cannot be trusted to select their own pastors, bishops, or delegates to General Conference. (The current system resembles how United States senators were elected before adoption of the Seventeenth Amendment to the United States Constitution in 1913. Before that, it was assumed the people could not be trusted to vote directly for their preferred candidate. They elected the people [state legislators] who had the authority to elect the senators. That expression of distrust of the people was discarded more than eighty years ago.)

Most of the "Made in America" religious traditions place a far higher level of trust in the laity. More important, this trust becomes the foundation for challenging congregational leaders, and the laity in general, to do what they know they cannot do.

One result is that at this fork in the road the churches that challenge doubters to become believers, believers to become disciples, and disciples to become apostles are more effective in reaching the generations born after 1955. They are more effective in turning atheists into missionaries. Likewise the churches that challenge the laity to create innovative new ministries to meet new needs, that challenge congregations to plant new missions, that challenge the creativity, participation, and gifts of the laity, and that trust people to respond are attracting huge numbers of newcomers.

By contrast, that path labeled Distrust is attracting fewer and fewer people.

Jerusalem or Athens?

Another fork in the road has received extensive publicity in the secular press in recent years as scholars debate the historicity of the life and ministry of Jesus.

A useful frame of reference for looking at this debate can be traced back nearly nineteen centuries to the lawyer, Tertullian, in Carthage. What is the road to truth? Reason as urged by the philosophers? Or the revelation of God in Christ?

More recently this has been described as the choice between Jerusalem, the city of faith, and Athens, the city of reason.

In academic terms in this country Christians founded colleges to help perpetuate the faith. As they became universities, many identified with Athens, rather than Jerusalem.[12] Currently the question is being raised whether the next generation of pastors should be educated in graduate schools of theology, that often are under tremendous pressures to be approved by the residents of Athens, or professional schools or teaching churches that have earned the endorsement of the residents of Jerusalem? Will your proposed restructure be designed for people from Athens or Jerusalem? Those who reply, "Both!" should recognize that we have very few models of "both" that average more than 300 at worship and have either a multicultural constituency or reach large numbers of people born after 1955.

Denomination or Seminary?

How does one particular religious tradition transmit the central tenets of that institutional expression of Christianity, the doctrines, the polity, and the denominational heritage from one generation to the next? One channel has been father-to-son as the son followed the father into the ordained ministry.

A second and overlapping system was illustrated by The Methodist Church. For more than a dozen decades, the number one Methodist channel was the annual conference. In the late-nineteenth and early-twentieth centuries, that was supplemented with an increased reliance on biblical institutes, theological seminaries, and divinity schools.

The twentieth century brought two forks in the road for Methodists and others as they headed toward the twenty-first century. The first is illustrated by The United Methodist Church. It was the decision to transform that relatively small, intimate, and clergy owned-and-operated religious gathering into a large, tightly scheduled, and anonymous business meeting called an annual conference. In 1906 the 5.2 million members of the six predecessor denominations were divided among 282 annual conferences. Ninety years later the 8.6 million members were divided among 67 annual conferences. The annual conferences no longer are designed to transmit from generation to generation a shared belief system nor a common denominational tradition.

The second change occurred in the theological schools. In a natural, normal, and predictable manner, most theological seminaries and university-related divinity schools have evolved from an earlier role as professional schools into academic institutions. A few even go so far as to identify themselves as graduate schools of theology. As academic institutions they become accountable, not to the churches nor to the regional judicatories served by their graduates, but rather to national and regional academic accrediting agencies. These accreditation agencies naturally use the traditional academic criteria of institutional inputs (proportion of faculty who have earned the Doctor of Philosophy degree, the number of scholarly articles and books published by each professor, the number of books in the library, the salary schedule, the ratio of professors-to-students, the size of the endowment fund, the benefits guaranteed the faculty such as tenure and sabbaticals and the adequacy of the physical plant).

By contrast, the churches use a different set of criteria to evaluate candidates interested in becoming their pastor. Is this person of good moral character? Does this candidate display a clear call from God? Does this candidate truly believe Jesus Christ is Lord and Savior? Is this candidate a persuasive preacher? Is this candidate a lucid communicator? Does this candidate bring a high level of competency in the skills required to be an effective pastor? Does this candidate really love people? It is unrealistic to expect a community of scholars to instill those qualities in a candidate for the ministry! It is realistic to expect that community of scholars will always be on the alert to identify students who have the qualities required to eventually join that community of scholars.

It is also unrealistic to expect twentieth-century theological seminaries and divinity schools to transmit a powerful denominational ethos. As Chicago Divinity School Dean W. Clark Gilpin has pointed out: "When the mainstream churches are actively seeking new avenues for reestablishing the vigor of denominational identities, they find the seminaries generally sympathetic but not much help."[13] Gilpin goes on in this provocative essay to describe the transformation of the theological seminary in the twentieth century.

Denominationalism has been increasingly perceived "as a problem to be overcome." Gender, race, and class have replaced the denominational tradition as the standard for defining one's personal religious identity. The transmission of denominational traditions under denominational doctrinal stance was replaced by the goal of making this a respectable scholarly discipline. The ideal faculty member is a scholar who has earned the respect of other scholars. Therefore it is unrealistic to expect the seminary to be able to train people to be effective parish pastors. The new criteria for a seminary became "urban," "ecumenical," and "university-related," rather than parish centered.

Money or Ministry?

What does the denominational system reward? One example of this fork in the road can be seen in two pieces of paper. The first identifies the five requirements to achieve the honor of being recognized as a "Five Star Church" in one United Methodist annual conference.

(1) Pay your World Service and Conference Benevolence apportionment in full.
(2) Give to one or more World Advance projects.
(3) Give to one or more National Advance projects.
(4) Give to one or more UMCOR projects.
(5) Give to one or more Conference Advance projects.

The second piece of paper defines the criteria for becoming a "Key Church" in the Baptist General Convention of Texas. A Key Church is expected to meet all six of these criteria.

(1) Makes a long-term commitment to make missions outreach a top priority.
(2) Prioritizes missions to the level of the church's religious education and music programs.
(3) Establishes a Missions Development council.

(4) Elects a director/minister of missions to lead missions expansion.

(5) Begins five mission/ministry units each year.

(6) Sponsors at least five dependent or pre-independent satellite units on a continuous basis.

Expectations do influence values, priorities, beliefs, and behavior!

Large or Small?

One indisputable pattern of the 1990s is that younger churchgoers can be found in disproportionately large numbers among the very large congregations founded since 1970.

This raises a significant fork in the road question for those charged with designing a new denominational structure. Should the new system be designed to increase the number of large congregations or to increase the number of small churches?

The Evangelical Free Church of America, the Lutheran Church-Missouri Synod, the Evangelical Covenant Church, the Evangelical Lutheran Church in America, and the Reformed Church in America are among the denominations designed to encourage the emergence of large churches. The Southern Baptist Convention has quadrupled the number of large churches since 1955. The Church of the Nazarene, which for many decades was a small church tradition, has intentionally increased the number of large congregations.

The Church of the Brethren, the Free Methodist Church of North America, and the Wesleyan Church are organized as small church traditions. (See table VII in the appendix.)

During the past three decades the operational policies of The United Methodist Church (appointments, apportionments, subsidies) have sharply increased the number and proportion of small congregations and reduced the number of larger churches. Between 1980 and 1994, for example, the number of congregations reporting an average worship attendance of fewer than 20 increased by 39 percent, despite the closing or merger of hundreds of very small congregations. (See table VI in the appendix.)

As you restructure your regional judicatory or national denominational system, will the design call for more large churches or more small congregations?

Regulate or Resource?

Sooner or later this question arises. What is the primary role of national denominational structures in relationship to (1) congregations and (2) regional judicatories?

The answer to that question can be found in the first four options of this chapter: If the central culture of the denomination is (a) structured around vertical lines of authority, (b) based on the assumption that institutions, not people, should be trusted, (c) designed to perpetuate a medieval European heritage, and (d) organized on the assumption that congregational leaders cannot be trusted, the answer is obvious. The number one responsibility of a denominational system is to regulate the role, behavior, and beliefs of individuals, congregations, and regional judicatories. This normally calls for a legalistic polity designed to facilitate permission-withholding. The system also will include provisions for appealing decisions to higher courts of the church. The denomination will determine the standards for ordination, the criteria for determining the final destination of financial contributions, the organizational structure for congregations, the role, responsibilities of regional judicatories, and a thousand other issues. Law moves ahead of grace.

Roman Catholics, Presbyterians, and United Methodists are three of the leading American examples of placing a high priority on the need for the larger denominational system to regulate with congregations and regional judicatories.

If, however, the core culture of that religious tradition emphasizes (a) horizontal lines, (b) trusting people, and (c) American democratic philosophy, the natural result is to focus on ministry and missional goals for both congregations and regional judicatories. That means the primary role of the national denominational system will be to resource congregations and regional judicatories. Grace moves ahead of law.

In recent years powerful forces in the Lutheran Church-Missouri Synod, the Southern Baptist Convention, the Episcopal Church, and the Evangelical Lutheran Church in America have been advocating a stronger regulatory role for the national denominational systems and, in some cases, the regional judicatory.

When the time comes to restructure a denominational system, a critical question is, "Should the new structure be designed to regulate or to resource?" It would be premature to respond to that question, however, without first discussing the forks in the road raised earlier in this chapter.

High Expectations or Low?

One 200-member congregation averages 800 at worship. Across the street is a 200-member congregation that averages 95 to 100 at worship. Sunday school attendance in the first church, including children in the nursery, averages 860. At the second church, Sunday school attendance averages 85 including three adult classes with eight to ten in each class. Approximately forty-five people participate in both Sunday school and worship in the second church.

What are the differences between those two congregations? One is age. The first congregation began meeting in 1972 and the founding pastor is the current senior minister. The second was founded in 1957 and has been served by eight ministers, each with a different approach to ministry.

The second congregation is affiliated with a denomination that retains a strong medieval European culture and places a premium on the regulatory role of the denomination. The first is affiliated with a "Made in America" religious tradition that is organized around the second person of the Trinity, evangelism, missions, and resourcing congregations.

The BIG difference, however, is that from day one the first congregation projected high expectations of people. It requires a thirty-six-week orientation course of anyone who contemplated seeking to become a member. Everyone is expected to participate in both Sunday school and worship every Sunday morning. By definition, all members are committed and trained volunteers. It is not irrelevant to note that (a) it became financially self-supporting 43 weeks after that first public worship service and (b) over the years 78 members have left to enter the full-time Christian ministry. One wall is covered with the portraits of these former members.

On all but eight or ten Sundays of the year a majority of the resident members of the second congregation either stay away from worship completely or go elsewhere to church. A two-hour orientation session is required of all prospective new members. It was not until 1976, nineteen years after it first began, that this congregation became fully financially self-supporting. Another denominational subsidy of $80,000 arrived nine years ago to help pay for construction of a modest addition to the meeting place.

Is the current culture of your denomination designed to encourage the emergence of high expectation churches or low expectation congregations? Will the new organizational structure be designed to undergird high expectation churches or to subsidize low expectation congregations?

That, however, introduces a related question for your restructuring process.

5.

WHAT'S IT ALL ABOUT?

One wall in a corridor of a church building in Texas features the large framed portraits of men who had been elected to the episcopacy while serving as the senior minister of that congregation.

A well traveled corridor in a church building in Georgia has both walls covered with framed photographs. One wall uses colored photographs to depict the meeting places of new congregations this church helped to create. The other wall features the framed colored pictures of houses this congregation constructed or rehabilitated in partnership with Habitat for Humanity. Both walls have conspicuously vacant spots for additional photographs.

The symbolism is clear. That wall in Texas sends the message that a high priority for a congregation is to provide skilled leadership for the denomination. Those two walls in Georgia send the message that missional outreach is a high priority for a congregation.

Which wall is most likely to inspire the first-time visitor from out of state to tell friends back home, "Let me tell you about the church we worshiped in while we were on vacation. On one wall they . . ."

It is not irrelevant to note that the Texas congregation, which provided excellent episcopal leaders for their denomination, experienced a 40 percent decline in worship attendance between 1965 and 1995. The Georgia congregation tripled in size during those years.

What is the number one priority for a congregation as we enter a new millennium? To provide leadership and financial support for the denominational system? Or to be engaged in evangelism and missional outreach? The answer depends on one's perspective. For some who look at the world from a national or regional denominational perspective, the priorities are clear. The national and regional expressions of that denomination have two urgent needs. One is money. The other is gifted, creative, effective, and future-oriented leaders. Congregations are expected to provide both. It is not irrelevant to note that two of the most important and widely debated issues when the national or regional denominational conventions are held are (1) the budget and (2) the election of new leaders.

It is not uncommon for the exceptionally effective pastor of an outstanding congregation to resign to accept a leadership office in the denominational system. It is less common for a highly competent leader in a denominational system to resign that office to become a parish pastor.

Does that suggest the primary role of congregations is to provide leadership and money for denominational systems? That is a normal, natural, and predictable perspective for anyone looking out of the window of a national denominational office.

This book is written from a different perspective. Instead of beginning with the needs of the denominational system, this observer contends any proposal for restructuring should center in on these three questions. In your judgment, are these the right questions?

Three Questions

(1) How do we create and resource congregations designed to live out the two great commandments of Jesus and to help fulfill the Great Commission?

(2) How do we transmit the Christian faith from one generation to the next?

(3) What is the role of the denominational system in fulfilling the Great Commission?

If these are the central questions to be raised in designing a denominational system, they suggest priorities. For example, which is the more important national denominational agency? The board of missions or the pension board? What should dominate the agenda in the business sessions of the national convention of that denomination? Choosing up sides over regulatory issues or designing a missional strategy? What are we looking for when we choose a leader for our denomination? A wagon master who can rally everyone to support missional causes and lead the denomination into the twenty-first century? Or an ideologue who enjoys forcing people to choose up sides on highly divisive issues? A leader who trusts people and operates on the assumption that when the laity are challenged to do what everyone knows cannot be done, the people will respond? Or someone who is more comfortable with a legalistic system based on distrust of people?

Or has the time come for both national and regional denominational agencies to move out of the medieval European vertical system of authority lines and redefine their role as servant organizations?[1]

If that is the preferred road to the twenty-first century, what changes must be made in the present denominational system to facilitate the emergence of servant leaders? Is that possible? Will that require beginning with a statement of what it is all about and then designing a system based on assumptions consistent with the servant approach to denominational leadership? Are the three questions raised earlier in this chapter a good beginning point for that discussion? Or should they be rearranged in a different sequence?

What Is Realistic?

A different, and more pragmatic approach to the question of the role of denominational agencies begins with three simple facts of life and an analogy.

The first simple fact is that in most denominations the vast majority of congregations founded before 1960 are either on a plateau in size or shrinking in numbers.

The second fact of life is that in most denominations the majority of congregations report an average worship attendance of fewer than eighty. (See table VIII in the appendix.) When that is linked to the widely shared assumption that an average worship attendance of at least 100 to 120 is required to (a) offer a full and challenging workload for a full-time, fully credentialed, and resident pastor, (b) encourage pastors to stay for more than seven years, and (c) provide an adequate compensation package for a pastor, an important question surfaces. At least a few will argue that number is 135 to 160, not 100 to 120 average worship attendance. How many full-time pastors are needed?

The third fact is churchgoers born after 1955 apparently prefer congregations that can mobilize the discretionary resources required to offer them meaningful and high quality choices in nurturing their spiritual journey.

For an analogy we turn to the question of why are public schools failing to educate many of their students. One critic, Stanley Pogrow, points out, "The equivalent of expecting teachers to develop the interventions they are going to apply (is) asking an actor to perform Shakespeare—but to write the play first."[2] Pogrow goes on to point out that in the practice of medicine, physicians who invent their own medical procedures are vulnerable to charges of malpractice.

In the parish ministry, however, we expect a minister to come in, invent the appropriate strategy for ministry for that particular congregation and also to implement that strategy. According to Pogrow, that makes as much sense as asking a physician to invent and apply the appropriate procedure for treating an illness or for a teacher to invent and implement the appropriate strategy for teaching algebra to a group of fifteen-year-olds or for a group of vocalists to first compose and next sing an anthem without a director, music, or rehearsals.

In other words, are we projecting completely unrealistic expectations when we ask a pastor who served a small county seat town church for eight years to come lead this hundred-year-old Anglo congregation in a racially changing neighborhood into a new era in its ministry?

Twelve Responses

One response is, "If 5 percent of the pastors can do that, why can't the other 95 percent?"

A second is, "The fault is with the seminaries. They do not train students to be effective pastors."

A third is, "That's why we need to concentrate on planting more new missions rather than waste resources trying to renew hundred-year-old dying churches."

A fourth is, "Perhaps if that pastor goes back to school for a Doctor of Ministry degree that will provide the skills required to lead that congregation into a new day."

A fifth is, "That's why denominational leaders should place ministers rather than allow congregations to call their own pastor. We can produce better matches between gifts and needs than can an unsophisticated call committee."

A sixth is, "If other churches would send us more money, we could finance the renewal of that hundred-year-old church."

A seventh is, "My advice is dissolve the congregation, sell the property to a black church, and use those funds to start a new mission to the underprivileged."

An eighth is, "The role of the denomination is to design, staff, and administer the workshop that will train that pastor and a group of volunteer leaders in how to become a multicultural congregation."

A ninth response is, "The basic problem is we are not attracting the truly gifted young people to go into the ministry. We need to go back and improve our recruitment system to attract the best and the brightest to the parish ministry."

A tenth is, "That minister should have been given the opportunity to serve a two or three year internship on the staff of a church that had successfully completed the transition to become a multicultural church before being asked to go into that situation. We require all our prospective church planters to serve on the staff of a very large church before going out to plant a new mission. That way we are able to plant new missions that usually are averaging at least 300 at worship by the end of the first year."

An eleventh response is, "The appropriate analogy is small business. Most small businesses fail within two years because they don't have a custom designed business or they're undercapitalized. That's why so many buy a franchise. The franchise holder takes over an ailing store and turns it around in twelve to eighteen months. We need to adapt the concept of the franchise to how we plant new missions or turn around dying churches. The role of the denomination would be to design a couple of dozen different franchise plans. One would be for the rural church located in what is now exurbia. Another for the aging downtown church.[3] A third would be for the dying Anglo church in a racially changing neighborhood. A fourth for new missions in growing suburban communities. A couple more would be for new missions in the large central cities.

"The denominational leaders would work with the leaders in each of these franchises to help perfect the design. After that has been accomplished, that church would be a partner with the denomination in training pastors for new franchises."

A twelfth response is, "We must affirm three basic assumptions as a beginning point: (a) the parish ministry is far more difficult and demanding than it was in the 1950s; (b) the parish ministry is far more competitive than it was as recently as the 1980s; (c) every congregation is a unique worshiping community in a unique environment. No two are alike.

"Next, we have to abandon the role of the denomination as a program agency with the dream that people from forty different churches can come to one big rally and all will benefit equally. We must replace that model with a highly skilled staff who will be in partnership with a network of teaching churches. One part of the process requires the staff to work with congregational leaders in designing a custom-made strategy to fit that particular church's resources and environment. Next, we must take the leadership from that congregation to a teaching church that has been implementing a similar strategy. This will enable them to learn from practitioners how to implement their strategy. In the ideal world the pastor who is serving a congregation that needs to define a new role for a new day will have spent a year or two, or at least a month or two, on the staff of a teaching church that resembled that one five years ago and now has moved into a new era in its history. To accomplish this, we need to make this model the top priority in the denominational strategy. We also need a variety of top quality teaching churches that model how to identify, reach, and serve a new constituency."

Which of these responses is most compatible with your present denominational structure? Which should be a motivating force in designing your new structure?

6.

WHAT ARE THE BEST STRATEGIES?

Sooner or later every restructuring process must resolve this question. Do we first design what we believe will be the ideal denominational structure for the twenty-first century and after we have completed that, we formulate a series of strategies for our regional judicatories and congregations that are consistent with that larger design? Or do we begin with formulating a series of strategies and subsequently design a denominational structure that will facilitate implementation of those strategies?

Do we choose an enticing organizational structure design path and let that choice determine our strategies? Or do we first choose our destination and then pick the road that will take us from here to there?

If the choice is to begin by formulating alternative strategies, here are a dozen to provoke your thinking.

The historical record suggests that among the most effective components of a larger and more comprehensive strategy are these twelve. Why twelve? Why not focus solely on planting new missions? Or on revitalizing long-established churches? One reason is the shortage of pastors with the gifts, skills, and experience required to implement any one of these twelve components of a larger strategy.

Pioneer the New

Start new churches and invite the members of these new generations and the new immigrants to help pioneer the creation of new worshiping communities. A reasonable estimate is no more than 10 percent of all pastors possess the gifts, skills, experience, and temperament to plant a new mission that will be averaging at least 500 at worship at the end of five years. That does place a ceiling on new church development, but a modest goal would be to launch each year a number equivalent to one percent of the present number of congregations in your denomination. Thus a denomination with 10,000 congregations would plant one hundred new missions annually. This would offset the natural annual death rate of seven to eight per 1000 congregations. An aggressive growth strategy calls for 2 percent annually. Several Protestant denominations are now averaging 3 to 4 percent annually.

Transform the Old

Encourage long-established congregations to design and implement a strategy that will enable them to double or triple or quadruple in size. This is a far more difficult strategy to implement than planting new missions. One reason for the difficulty is that requires persuading the members to change local traditions and cultures and to "do church differently." A second reason is it requires a far higher level of skill in the pastor who is leading this effort.

Planting a new church requires a far above average level of ministerial skill in four areas—evangelism, preaching, institution-building, and leadership development. A reasonable estimate is that 15 percent of all pastors, if they are convinced this is their call, have the competence to plant a new mission that will be averaging at least 350 in worship by the end of three years.

While it is risky to place too much weight on any one factor, several recent surveys of the pastors who have been most effective in planting new missions or in revitalizing long-established churches come in disproportionately large numbers from among those who carry either the ENTJ or ESTJ profile on the Myers-Briggs Type Indicator.

By contrast, introducing and implementing a church growth strategy in a long numerically declining congregation usually requires a very high level of ministerial competence in nine areas—evangelism, preaching, initiating planned change from within an organization, the transformation of old institutions, building a leadership coalition that includes both (a) longtime members with a strong attachment to the past and to local traditions and (b) members who are driven by the combination of a powerful future-orientation, a deep commitment to outreach, persistence, innovative program development, and fund-raising. A reasonable estimate is between 5 and 10 percent of all pastors display a high level of competence in all of those areas.

Relocate

While this is often a combination of the first two, a third strategy is to encourage congregations to relocate and design a new ministry plan to reach new generations of people. Usually this is easier to implement than either of the first two, *if the members can be persuaded to adopt it*, since it includes: (a) beginning with substantial resources; (b) specific, attainable, measurable, and highly visible goals; and (c) by the fact the people voted to relocate, a group of people committed to change. This strategy does not require the very high level of skills in the pastor that is required in the first two, but it usually does work best with a pastorate of at least fifteen years.

Implementation of this alternative would call for an average of 1 to 2 percent of all congregations annually to relocate their meeting place as part of a larger strategy to design a new role for a new era to reach new generations. Perhaps 20 percent of all pastors, given the appropriate appointment and a tenure of at least fifteen years, are equipped to lead a successful relocation effort. This would be an essential component of any strategy to achieve the goal that, by the year 2010, 8 to 10 percent of all congregations would be averaging more than 350 at worship.

One approach to a national denominational strategy is to seek to have a denominational presence in as many different places as possible, even though most of these will be small congregations. A different strategy is to encourage the emergence of more very large churches. One example of the contrasting results between those two strategies is the nine largest Evangelical Lutheran Church in America parishes report a combined average worship attendance of approximately 25,000—the same as the combined worship attendance of the 979 smallest ELCA congregations. (See table X in the appendix for additional examples.)

A Good Succession

The most subtle and the most cost-effective strategy is to create a smooth and productive transition when the senior pastor of the very large congregation retires, resigns, or dies. Too often a poorly designed transition results in a substantial numerical decline. For example, in 1965 sixty-three Methodist congregations reported an average worship attendance of 1,100 or more. Sixty percent of them reported at least a 40 percent decrease in worship attendance over the next thirty years. In most of them that decline followed the arrival of a new senior minister. Was that simply a coincidence?

In several other American religious traditions, and in many independent churches, the response to that syndrome has been to identify the probable successor several years in advance and invite that person to join the staff as the associate pastor. Five or ten years later, that potential successor begins to fully understand the distinctive culture of that congregation and has had the time and the opportunities to earn the trust of the members and to build relationships with the other persons on the paid staff. One version of this scenario calls for the associate minister to pick up one-fifth of the senior pastor's workload in year one of a five-year transitional period, two-fifths in the second year, three-fifths in the third year, and four-fifths in the fourth year.

Another design calls for building teams. Instead of a staff configuration headed by a senior minister, this design calls for a team of five persons. Typically two or three share the preaching and teaching responsibilities. One also directs the program team, one also leads the administrative staff, one also leads the worship team, one relates to the elders and deacons, and one is responsible for community outreach. These team leaders constitute the executive staff. When one departs, the resulting hole is only 20 to 30 percent the size in the traditional configuration following the departure of the senior pastor. This arrangement means the continuity is in that team, not in one person. It also enables the remaining four members of the team to socialize the new staff member into the culture of that congregation as well as into how that team functions.

This design is based on a twofold generalization. First, the smaller the size of the congregation, the more likely the continuity with the past will be found in the members, in local traditions, in the real estate, in the denominational affiliation, and in the volunteer leadership. By contrast, the larger the size of the congregation, the more likely the continuity will be in the ministry, in the pastor, and in the program staff.

A third response to the issue of succession in the very large church is to confine the search for a new senior minister to persons who have been serving as the associate pastor in a congregation with a similar culture and of approximately the same size or, preferably, somewhat larger.

In several denominations the polity prohibits use of the first two of these alternatives.

Resource for Change

In recent years, state conventions in the Southern Baptist Convention, districts in the Lutheran Church-Missouri Synod, dioceses in the Episcopal Church, and other regional judicatories have been developing another strategy to reach new generations and new immigrants.[2]

This calls for transforming the regional judicatory from its old role as a program and ministerial placement agency into a new and more demanding role. The new role has five major components:

(a) working with individual congregations, and occasionally with clusters of churches, in designing a customized strategy for that particular congregation; (b) challenging both congregations and individuals to venture beyond their self-imposed limitations in launching new ministries and new expressions of Christian outreach; (c) helping the congregation translate that strategy into a customized ministry plan; (d) resourcing congregations to enable them to implement that customized ministry plan; and (e) helping congregations and/or small clusters of pastors to create learning communities.[3]

One example of the changes required to implement this alternative are illustrated by The United Methodist Church. This would require: (a) a redefinition of the role of the annual conference, (b) a redefinition of the role of the district superintendent, (c) the adoption of new criteria for the selection of superintendents, (d) the appropriate training for new superintendents, (e) extending the tenure of superintendents from ten to thirty years, and (f) a change in the evaluation system. Instead of evaluating congregations and pastors on the basis of the percentage of apportionments paid, this would mean evaluating the annual conference and the district superintendents on the success of congregations in implementing their ministry plan.

Similarly Presbyterians would need to redefine the role of the presbytery and Lutherans would need to redefine the role of the synod or district staff.

The Church Within a Church

One of the most attractive of these twelve alternatives often is described as "a church within a church." The full-time pastor of a congregation averaging 60 to 150 at worship first earns the trust of the people and subsequently seeks permission to launch a new ministry with people that congregation has been unable to reach. One example is the aging white congregation and the pastor who secures permission to launch a new off-campus mission that will be designed to reach young adults. They meet for worship on Saturday evening in another facility (the advantage of a neutral site with no barriers to strangers). Within a year or two this becomes a self-expressing, self-governing, self-propagating, and self-financing new ministry. A few years later those members may decide to merge with that aging congregation, or they may choose to become a new congregation. A parallel is when the pastor of the small white congregation, that today includes few members who live within two miles of the meeting place, launches a new ministry to reach the new residents of that racially changing neighborhood.

Given the appropriate match between pastors and congregation, and a tenure of at least seven or eight years, perhaps 40 percent of all pastors could be encouraged to implement this strategy.

Renew the Old

A popular and widely acclaimed strategy is to find the pastor who can come in and revitalize a long-established congregation that has been experiencing several years of numerical decline. Successful implementation of this strategy requires, (a) the highest level of competence in the pastor of any of these nine alternatives, and (b) a long pastorate of at least a dozen years. This strategy usually is designed either to (a) reach new generations of people from that same meeting place or (b) reach several different slices of the population in terms of race, language, age, ethnicity, social class, education, or income levels.

The historical record suggests that with the appropriate match between the needs of the congregation and the skills of the pastor, and a tenure of at least seven to ten years, perhaps 3 percent of all parish ministers are equipped to translate this dream into reality. For most congregations and most pastors it is far easier to make a fresh start at a new location. From a denominational perspective it usually is more effective and less expensive to plant new missions to reach these segments of the population.

Off-Campus Ministries

Encourage existing congregations with discretionary resources to launch off-campus ministries to reach people who, (a) would not enter that intimidating building housing the congregation, or (b) represent a substantially different slice of the population (university students, new immigrants from Asia, rural residents coming to a large city), or (c) cannot be accommodated in the present meeting place because of the limitations of space.

Currently no more than 10 percent of all American Protestant congregations possess the discretionary resources required to implement this strategy. In addition, in several denominations the polity is not supportive of this strategy. Far more significant, however, this strategy works best when the denomination, the regional judicatory, and the congregation all are organized around the twin goals of evangelism and missions.

This strategy can be most effective when combined with (a) the redefinition of the role of the regional judicatory described earlier and (b) the leadership of a minister of missions who is on the staff of the church engaged in off-campus ministries.[4]

Reproduce and Grow

Encourage larger congregations and/or coalitions of congregations to plant new churches.

This is not compatible with the current polity of several denominations that place the authority for starting new congregations in the denominational system. This strategy, however, is widely used in parts of American Protestantism, and several ELCA parishes are now "mothering" new congregations. At least one-half of all the new missions launched in the 1990s will be initiated by (a) individual congregations, (b) clusters of churches, (c) entrepreneurial individuals, or (d) a small group of deeply committed Christian volunteers. This alternative is most attractive when the ecclesiastical system displays unreserved trust in the laity and also is designed to challenge both individuals and congregations to do what they know they cannot do.

The Teaching Church

The easiest to implement of these twelve alternatives already is beginning to happen. This is the emergence of self-identified teaching churches and was referred to earlier. These are congregations with a high level of competence in one or more areas of ministry (reaching single young adults, relocation of the meeting place, transforming the congregation into a learning community, ministries with families with new babies, building a multicultural community, transforming believers into disciples and disciples into apostles, functioning as a multisite congregation). They invite leaders from other congregations to learn from their experiences.

Adopt the Independents

Adopt independent churches who are seeking a denominational home. While this has been a central component of the strategy of a couple of mainline denominations, it has yet to be given serious consideration by most denominations and can produce considerable conflict, especially if the adopted congregation seeks substantial financial subsidies as the primary reason for seeking adoption.

Training

This is placed last because the research on training programs suggests most have limited effectiveness. Experience does suggest, however, that intensive, narrowly focused, three-to-twelve week, demanding, and field-based (as contrasted with classroom) training experiences can produce substantial improvements in the level of competency of at least one-third of the participants.

One Alternative: Grow Old

The inability of the present system in several denominations to choose and implement a strategy to reach new generations has meant that gradually an increasing proportion of that shrinking inventory of members is drawn from adults born before 1945. Many of the present systems, including the adult Sunday school, the financial support of the denomination, and securing delegates to attend denominational conventions are heavily dependent on people born before 1950. The average age of lay delegates to the 1996 General Conference of The United Methodist Church, for example, was 59 years, up from 55.6 years in 1988.

The big positive consequence, of course, is that this concentration on older, Anglo, and financially well-to-do Americans has provided a comparatively strong financial base. The most generous financial contributors to the churches, both Roman Catholic and Protestant, are persons age fifty and over. This has allowed thousands of congregations and dozens of regional judicatories to postpone making difficult decisions. The generous financial support of these longtime and remarkably loyal members also has enabled both denominational agencies and congregations to perpetuate old systems and old agendas for the last third of the twentieth century.

A second positive consequence is that the current membership of several denominations includes millions of adults who grew up in an era that taught them to trust big institutions.

A United Methodist Detour

At this point a couple of United Methodist readers may pause and ask, "Since you're a United Methodist adherent, which of these twelve alternative strategies should The United Methodist Church adopt and implement as it seeks to reach new generations and new immigrants with the good news of Jesus Christ?"

The answer, and a central thesis of this book, is that this question is premature. While it is a crucially important question that will determine the future of this denomination, it is pointless to discuss it now.

In sequential terms, another question must be raised first. Who has the authority to design a strategy and to mobilize the resources to implement it?

The answer today can be expressed in two words. **No one.**

Why does this vacuum of leadership exist today? One answer is the highly decentralized organizational structure that provides a hostile environment for leadership, initiative, responsibility, and accountability. Another is that contemporary leaders are unwilling to be held accountable or to lead. A third answer is the climate of distrust. A fourth is that the absence of clearly and precisely defined and widely supported denomination-wide goals make it impossible for leaders to lead. If there is no general agreement on the destination, which direction does the wagon master point to at sunrise? The current denominational agenda has been expanded to the point that it is impossible to win agreement on direction or priorities.

But rather than pursue that detour, let us return to the main road and look at an issue that many prefer to pretend does not exist.

7.

WHAT ARE THE TRADE-OFFS?

One of the great disappointments of my adult life has been the discovery that eating a bowl of ice cream while watching the late night news may not be the best strategy for losing weight. Research that has yet to be funded may disprove that conclusion, but contemporary evidence all points in the same direction. This illustrates the concept of a trade-off: The real choice may be between eating ice cream and losing weight.

The great Reformation that tore apart the Christian church in western Europe in the middle of the second millennium was about doctrine and theology. It also was about power, polity, the role of the ordinary person, control, the redistribution of wealth, trade-offs, leadership, nationalism, a dying feudal culture, evangelism, music, easy access to the Holy Scriptures, and the usefulness of old wineskins. One of the trade-offs was that when the common people gained access to the Scripture, it no longer would be possible for a single religious tradition to dominate the life of a country, much less the entire continent.

More recently, the issue of trade-offs is illustrated by the aggressive affirmation of multiculturalism in Canada. It should be noted, first of all, that in at least two dozen areas of life, Canadians have pioneered new concepts ten to thirty years before they became popular south of the border. That list ranges from open immigration to privatization to metropolitan government to church union.

The current trade-off is between the desire for a united Canada and the dream of sovereign provinces. One result is the national birthday, which is celebrated on July 4 in the United States, is celebrated in Quebec on June 24 and by the English-speaking provinces on July 1. How can a nation be united without a shared sense of a common history and culture?

This book is largely about polity; natural, normal, and predictable patterns of institutional behavior; planned change initiated from within an institution; expectations; changing societal trends; assumptions about contemporary reality; choices; leadership; changing agendas; competition; obsolescence, and the need for new wineskins; but most of all, it is about the need for trust.

It is not the intent of this book to attempt to resolve that increasingly divisive issue of "confessionalism" versus "theological pluralism." That is being addressed by other writers in many other places.[1] That debate cannot be ignored completely because the outcomes will have a huge impact on the design of a denominational strategy. Will your denominational identity come from Jerusalem or Athens? The heart of this chapter, however, concerns the compatibility of goals, and that raises the issue of trade-offs.

The beginning point for this discussion is around expectations. Many congregations project very high expectations of people. One example is that high threshold for membership. In many high expectation congregations eligibility for seeking full membership may include: (1) regular participation in the corporate worship of God (that often means a minimum of once or twice a week); (2) participation in a 25-to-45 week class for prospective new members; (3) an active role in a continuing small group; (4) a commitment to tithing; and (5) involvement in a systematic training program designed to prepare people to use their gifts in ministry.

By contrast, the low expectation churches with a low threshold for membership may ask no more of those seeking to become members than one to four hours in an orientation class for prospective new members.

With perhaps a half dozen exceptions most mainline Protestant denominations do not project high expectations of people. The frequency of worship attendance by the members often is not much higher than it is for the adult population of the nation, age eighteen and over, including all the self-identified atheists, agnostics, doubters, and inactive believers.

One exception is the formal education requirement for ordination. A second is the expectation that all congregations can continue to flourish in an increasingly competitive ecclesiastical marketplace. A third is the proportion of total receipts congregations should be expected to allocate to support the denominational system. A fourth exception is the expectation for church members to participate in denominational rallies. A fifth high expectation is the size of the compensation package small congregations are expected to be able to provide their pastor. A sixth exception consists of perhaps 20 percent of all mainline Protestant congregations that have a high threshold for membership and/or project very high expectations of the laity and/or report a ratio of worship attendance-to-membership that exceeds 90 percent.

This is a factor to be reckoned with in designing a denominational strategy. Should that strategy be based on the projection of high expectations of people? Or on projecting low expectations? To design a high expectation strategy will require either a radical change in the denominational culture or an acceptance of disappointment when some of these high expectations are not fulfilled.

This can be illustrated by the trade-offs in three contemporary ideological goals.

Theological Pluralism

The first ideological goal reflects the desires of those who support the dream of *theological* pluralism. One expression of that dream calls for a highly pluralistic denomination including congregations scattered all along the theological spectrum from conservative to liberal. That is relatively easy to accommodate in a congregational polity in which each congregation, district, conference, and churchwide agency is granted unreserved autonomy. The United Church of Christ and the National Association of Congregational Christian Churches are two examples of a polity that can accommodate a high degree of theological pluralism. In other words, one trade-off is a closely knit and hierarchical connectional system of polity is not compatible with a high level of theological pluralism.

Far, far more difficult, however, is implementation of the dream that *every congregation* will be a theologically pluralistic fellowship. This observer's experience suggests four environments in which this is most likely to occur.

(1) The most common is the small congregation organized around the combination of a personable, loving, gregarious, caring, and extroverted long-tenured pastor and a high priority to living out the second of Jesus' two great commandments.[2]

(2) Less common is the larger congregation with an annual turnover rate below 6 percent in the membership led by an exceptionally competent and long-tenured pastor who is a superb listener and chooses life-situation sermon themes over expository preaching.

(3) The most attractive to younger generations is the very large congregation with an exceptionally creative program staff that is able to offer a rich range of choices in a seven-day-a-week ministry with two or three *different* worship experiences offered every weekend and at least two different preachers every weekend.

(4) The model of theological pluralism that satisfies many mature adults who are second or third or fourth generation members of that congregation is organized around a long-tenured pastor who is a loving shepherd, excels in one-to-one relationships, and does *not* project high expectations of the members. On forty Sundays out of every year, at least one-half of the members stay away from worship or go elsewhere to church.

Cultural Diversity

The second of these three ideological goals is articulated by those who long to see the day when every congregation will represent a high level of *cultural* diversity by drawing people together from a variety of ethnic, educational, nationality, social class, racial, generational, income, and occupational categories. This dream calls for the membership of a worshiping community to represent a cross section of the population of that community. Here we can identify five categories of congregations that have turned that dream into reality.

(1) The most highly visible are the spirit-filled congregations composed of self-identified charismatic Christians led by a charismatic pastor.

(2) A smaller number are not charismatic, but are led by an exceptionally competent pastor, often with a spouse who was reared in a different culture. These usually reflect a more limited degree of cultural diversity.

(3) The most common are the small congregations averaging fifteen to eighty-five at worship and organized as a network of one-to-one relationships with a personable, loving, and long-tenured pastor at the hub of that network (who often has a spouse with a good job to support that family).

(4) A third, and fairly large group is composed of congregations that project very high expectations of those who seek to become members. On the typical weekend their worship attendance is three to six times their membership.

(5) The last example resembles the third type described earlier with a rich range of high attractive choices for all ages in a seven-day-a-week ministry and three or more *different* worship experiences every weekend.

Completely Inclusive

A third and smaller group of leaders articulate the dream that some day their denomination will be widely known for both its theological pluralism *and* cultural diversity. One working model of that today is the Southern Baptist Convention which (1) is organized around missions and evangelism; (2) strongly affirms complete congregational autonomy; (3) affirms the homogeneity and autonomy of individual congregations, but displays an exceptionally high level of cultural diversity within the membership of the denomination; (4) includes congregations scattered all along the right half of the theological spectrum from fundamentalist to middle-of-the-road *but nearly all of them exalt the second person of the Trinity*; (5) has been able to survive considerable conflict within the national level by rallying state convention, associational, and congregational leaders around the twin goals of missions and evangelism; (6) has been able to avoid most of the distractions of the ecumenical movement of the last third of the twentieth century; (7) has experienced remarkable success in reaching members of ethnic minority groups in the large central cities by planting many new missions designed for a clearly defined slice of the population; (8) encourages congregations with discretionary resources to launch many off-campus ministries staffed by trusted and trained lay volunteers; (9) strongly endorses pioneering new ways of doing ministry; (10) has expanded its ministries with recent immigrants to include churches that now worship in a total of 106 different languages; and (11) affirms the concept of dual affiliation whereby one congregation can be a member of two different denominations.

If the focus of this dream is shifted from a denominational system with a high degree of internal cultural diversity and theological pluralism to individual congregations, three kinds of congregations represent fulfillment of that dream of theological pluralism *and* cultural diversity.

(1) The most common is the small church served by a long-tenured pastor who is widely viewed as a "maverick," who genuinely cares for people and continually challenges members with big dreams. In addition, these congregations live out the concept of participatory worship, affirm the leadership of the laity, give high visibility to and repeatedly publicly affirm their own custom-designed missional statement that emphasizes inclusion rather than exclusion, recognize the power of locally created rituals that reinforce that congregation's distinctive identity, place a high premium on relationships, communicate the gospel clearly to persons born after World War II, affirm the value of single function task forces

over a network of standing committees, are comfortable with an ad hoc approach to ministry, accept the fact that it is unreasonable to expect that everyone will hold the same position on any one issue of public policy, can live comfortably without a surplus in the monthly financial report, truly expect and actively welcome first-time visitors at every public worship service, reward creativity by individuals, do not feel driven by either denominational or local traditions, and give a high priority to ministries with children. The Park Slope United Methodist Church in Brooklyn, New York is one example of a congregation that, to a remarkable degree, combines theological pluralism with cultural diversity. The Edgehill United Methodist Church in Nashville, Tennessee is another example.

(2) Less common is the large congregation served by a long-ten-ured ordained minister who is an exceptionally effective communicator, an outstanding teacher in the pulpit and who understands the value of a talented program staff who can build and operate a seven-day-a-week ministry that is sensitive and responsive to a variety of personal human and spiritual needs. Most of these congregations schedule two or three or four *different* worship experiences every weekend.

(3) For many the ideal model of the church that combines theological pluralism with cultural diversity is the one that effectively challenges the laity to be engaged in doing off-campus ministries, provides the appropriate high quality training experiences for volunteers, depends on paid staff to administer "the business" of the parish, and provides regular inspirational events to undergird the ministry of the laity. These congregations rank at the top of that list of very high expectation churches. The potentially divisive nature of discussions on theological pluralism are pushed to the bottom of the agenda by the focus on missions. Likewise, the cultural differences among the participants quickly fade into insignificance as people work together in doing ministry in off-campus settings.

A common criticism of these congregations is that they are staff led rather than lay led. That is a dumb criticism! A central reason for why they work is that they are staff led!.

One of their responses to the tensions that often are produced by pluralism and diversity is an unreserved welcome to everyone who wants to participate, but clearly articulated requirements for anyone who seeks to become a full member. A common result is a worship attendance that exceeds the reported membership by a three or four or five to one ratio.

In simple terms, those goals of theological pluralism and cultural diversity are attainable, but they are not easy to sustain!

These models are offered here to illustrate a few of the trade-offs that will confront anyone responsible for designing a new denominational strategy.

(At this point we ask the reader's indulgence while we take another short detour, but you are welcome to read along.)

Another United Methodist Detour

(1) Is the current UMC operational policy of increasing the proportion of congregations that average fewer than thirty-five at worship compatible with the goal of reaching younger generations?

(2) Is the historic emphasis on short pastorates (three to ten years) compatible with the goal of (a) creating theologically pluralistic congregations and/or (b) creating culturally diverse congregations?

(3) Is the centralized control and command connectional polity consistent with encouraging theological pluralism and/or cultural diversity?

(4) Is the institutional distrust of congregational leadership compatible with reaching the generations born after World War II who, as a group, tend to distrust big institutions?

(5) Is the culture of a low expectation religious system, which tends to be reinforced by short pastorates, compatible with encouraging the emergence of more large congregations?

(6) Is the expectation that congregations will support and help fulfill denominational goals consistent with the dream of revitalizing goalless congregations that are drifting into the future?

(7) Can a denominational system that subsidizes mediocrity in ministerial leadership expect to produce the high level of competence among pastors that is required to fulfill a high expectation denominational strategy?

(8) Can a denominational system that has closed 40,000 churches in the past hundred years be expected to have a high level of competence in starting new churches?

(9) Can a denominational system designed to reach and serve people born before 1940 reach the generations born after 1955?

(10) Perhaps most important, can a denominational system organized on the principle of distrust of the laity, challenge and train lay volunteers to be engaged in community outreach ministries and in evangelism? Should trusting the local leadership and resourcing congregations replace the current regulatory role as the number one purpose of the districts and conferences?

(11) Can a religious tradition that carries a strong medieval European heritage be expected to reach large numbers of people who trace their ancestry back to Africa or to Asia?

(12) Finally, to return to an earlier theme, if a denominational system is in a state of denial, is it reasonable to expect that it will be able to confront and resolve these and similar issues that involve trade-offs between conflicting values and goals?

8.

WHAT IS CONTEMPORARY REALITY?

A useful planning model consists of three questions. In congregational use, the first question asks, "What is God calling this congregation to be and to be doing in the years ahead? The second question is, "What is contemporary reality?" The third question is, "Now that we agree on our destination and on where we are today, how do we get from here to there?"

A parallel model for a restructuring committee would first ask, "What will be the primary role of our national agencies and our regional judicatories in the early years of the third millennium? What does God expect of us as a distinctive religious tradition under the Christian umbrella? What is our distinctive responsibility in helping to build the kingdom of God on earth?"

The group discussing the future of the Southern Baptist Convention probably will not come to the same definition of a future role as will the task force responsible for recommending a new organizational structure for the Evangelical Lutheran Church in America. Therefore we will not chase that rabbit any farther in this chapter.

Is the Glass Half Full or Half Empty?

The second step often is more difficult because of the varied perspectives of the people in the room. Several may want to begin that description of contemporary reality by identifying strengths, resources, and assets. Another person may want to begin by focusing on problems, limitations, and liabilities. Either beginning point usually moves the discussion into highly subjective areas such as morale, commitment, blame, theological stance, public image, the competence of the denominational staff, and the apparent passion for evangelism.

A third alternative is to look at a couple of dozen denominational trends. Together these can provide an objective basis for describing the direction this denomination has been traveling in recent years. Once that direction has been defined, it will be relatively easy to determine the type and degree of change that will be required to move in a new direction to match the role that was articulated in that first step. A modest advantage of this reliance on trends is that occasionally useful comparisons can be made with other religious traditions.

To illustrate this approach to describing contemporary reality, we will look at The United Methodist Church. One reason for that choice is, along with the Lutheran Church-Missouri Synod, The United Methodist Church has accumulated a large quantity of high quality and internally consistent data covering several decades.

United Methodist Trends

(1) The number of congregations has decreased from 57,087 in the six predecessor denominations in the United States in 1906 to 36,559 at the end of 1994. When the new congregations are added to those totals, this denomination has lost an average of one church a day through dissolution or merger for the past one hundred years.

(2) The number of members has dropped from 11 million in 1968 to 8.6 million at the close of 1994. From the end of 1965 to the end of 1995, the *net* loss in membership has averaged nine per

hour for twenty-four hours a day, 365 days a year for thirty years! In 1960 the two predecessor denominations, exclusive of intradenominational transfers, received an average of 1400 new members every day. In 1994 the comparable daily figure was 810.

(3) The proportion of members-to-population declined in every one of the fifty states and in the District of Columbia, between 1960 and 1990. (See table II in the appendix.)

(4) The actual number of members decreased in 39 of the 50 states, and in the District of Columbia between 1960 and 1994.

(5) In 1956, when the number of live births in the United States was 4.2 million, the number of baptisms in the two predecessor denominations was nearly 440,000. In 1993, when the number of live births in the United States was slightly over 4 million, the number of baptisms was 161,000.

(6) The annual death rate for members of the Methodist Church as recently as 1964 was 7.4 per 1,000 members, considerably lower than for the American population, age 14 and over. While the death rate for the American population, age 14 and over, has been dropping, in 1994 the death rate for United Methodist Church members was 14.2 per 1,000, up from 12.6 in 1980. (See table III in the appendix.) Has the time arrived for every annual conference to offer driver education classes for mature members?

(7) The number of new members received on profession of faith (and restored) has plunged from nearly 400,000 annually in the two predecessor denominations in the late 1950s and early 1960s to 191,000 in 1994.

(8) The number of members received by intradenominational letters of transfer has dropped from approximately 320,000 annually in the late 1950s to 131,000 in 1994. Why do so many of those leaving a United Methodist congregation no longer choose another UM church?

(9) The number of new members received by letter of transfer from churches of other denominations has dropped from well over 100,000 annually in the late 1950s and early 1960s to 81,240 in 1994.

(10) During the six-year period of 1952 to 1958, exclusive of intradenominational transfers, nearly 2.9 million individuals joined a congregation affiliated with one of the two predecessor denominations. Losses totaled approximately 2.3 million for a net grain of slightly over 600,000.

During the recent six years from the end of 1988 through 1994, UM congregations received a total of nearly 1.7 million new members, again exclusive of interdenominational transfers. Losses came to 2.2 million for a net loss of a half million during these six years.

(11) Sunday morning worship in the two predecessor denominations averaged slightly over 4.3 million in 1965 and 3.4 million in 1994.

(12) Average Sunday school attendance was slightly over 4.1 million in the 1955–65 era and 1.8 million in 1994.

(13) Membership in the women's organizations dropped from nearly 2 million in 1960 to under one million in 1994.

(14) A recent and rarely discussed trend is the shrinking in the number of "entry level jobs" for recent seminary graduates. Frequently a recent seminary graduate is appointed to serve a congregation averaging between 100 and 199 at worship. The number of those congregations decreased by 6.7 percent in only three years.

(15) This long-term trend in reducing the total number of congregations, from 38,417 in 1980 to 36,559 in 1994, and in increasing the number of very small congregations reporting fewer than 35 at worship, from 9,897 in 1980 to 11,764 in 1994, has been accompanied by an increase in the number of ministers in "full connection" (active elders) from 30,877 in 1980 to 33,528 in 1994. This means an increasing financial burden on the annual conferences to subsidize jobs for full-time and fully credentialed clergy.

(16) This financial burden has increased as the number of retired clergy has grown from 7,103 in 1972 to 9,223 in 1980 to 13,260 in 1994. Some are covered by a fully funded pension system, but many are not.

(17) This next diagnostic comment is based on the assumption that every system produces the result it is designed to produce. For

THE SHRINKING MIDDLE

Distribution of UM Congregations by

Average Worship Attendance 1991–1994

Average Attendance	1991	1994	Change
1-19	4,773	5,668	+ 885
20-99	21,004	20,743	– 261
100-199	6,622	6,174	– 448
200-499	3,428	3,332	– 96
500+	569	604	+ 35

Number of congregations reporting average attendance 1991
= 36,396   (98.1%)
Number of congregations reporting average attendance 1994
= 36,521   (99.9%)
Change in total number of congregations from 37,100 in 1991 to 36,559 in 1994 or a decrease of 541—an average net loss of 180 congregations annually.

example, when early American Methodism gradually evolved from a missionary movement to a denomination, in 1819 the system produced the missionary society. More recently, when the United Methodist agenda became overloaded with a variety of new demands and causes, the system produced the Good News Movement (the Forum for Scriptural Christianity, Inc.) and the Mission Society for United Methodists as the modern day equivalent of the Mission Society of 1819.

Since the merger of 1968, The United Methodist Church appointment system apparently has been designed to produce more small congregations and fewer very large churches. (See tables IV, V, and VI in the appendix.) Between 1972 and 1994 the number of UM congregations reporting an average worship attendance of 200 or more dropped from 4,221 to 3,936. The proportion reporting fewer than 35 at worship grew from 25.6 percent in 1972 to 32.2 percent in 1994.

This pro–small church bias is highly visible when comparisons are made with other denominations. In eight of sixteen denominations 15 percent to 28 percent of all congregations report an average worship attendance of 200 or more. (See table VII.) For the UMC that proportion was 11 percent in 1994. In eleven of these sixteen denominations the median size was an average worship attendance between 70 and 124. (See table VIII.) The UMC was one of four in which the median size is under 60 at worship. This pro-small church bias of the UMC is even more pronounced if the focus is narrowed to very small congregations averaging fewer than 20 at worship. (See table IX.) In other denominations somewhere between 1 and 9 percent of all congregations report an average worship attendance of fewer than 210. The UM proportion is slightly over 15 percent.

Is your denominational structure based on the assumption that the generations born after 1955 will prefer small churches?

(18) How easy is it for a denomination to reverse a long-term effort to downsize? One expression of the downsizing syndrome in The United Methodist Church is in the reduction in the number of annual conferences from 282 in 1906 to 93 in 1965 to 73 in 1975 to perhaps 63 by 1999.

(19) One of the most significant long-term trends has been the withdrawal of this denomination from the large cities of the North and West such as Boston, New York, Philadelphia, Pittsburgh, Cleveland, Detroit, Chicago, Milwaukee, Madison, Des Moines, Denver, San Francisco, and Los Angeles.

(20) An overlapping trend has been the withdrawal from the Midwest and the West Coast. (See table II.) Between 1960 and 1990 UM membership decreased by 227,000 in Ohio, 183,000 in Pennsylvania, 180,000 in Illinois, 152,000 in Indiana, 114,000 in California, 109,000 in New York, 104,000 in Michigan, 103,000 in West Virginia, and 97,000 in Iowa.

(21) Perhaps one of the two or three most significant long-term trends, and the primary reason for the aging and shrinking of the membership, has been the reduction in new church development.

During the 1880s the predecessor denominations started an average of close to a thousand new missions annually. By the 1950s that had dropped to slightly under 200 annually. In the early 1970s the annual average was fewer than thirty, and in the 1990s it is less than a hundred. If the goal is to remain on a plateau in size and/or to reach younger generations and/or to reach recent immigrants and/or to become a multicultural denomination and/or to once again become a significant presence in the large central cities, that total must be increased to 300 to 600 annually. An annual average of 600 would be well under one-half the current Southern Baptist pace.

(22) The number of newly ordained elders (fully credentialed ministers) increased from an annual average of slightly over 700 in the early 1970s to well over 800 in the early and mid-1980s. In recent years that total has dropped to under 700 and was 670 in 1994. Given the sharp decline in the number of congregations that can both afford and justify a full-time and fully credentialed pastor, that means (a) a surplus or (b) an abundance of pastors to plant new churches.

(23) One piece of good news is that when compared to other denominations this is still a comparatively wealthy denomination. This is reflected in the compensation of the clergy, in the subsidies for smaller congregations, in the pension benefits, in the budgets of annual conferences, in the amount of money allocated for a variety of denominational meetings, in the fact that in 1995 the General Board of Global Ministries was able to contribute a total of $11.1 million to well over 600 organizations that are not formally part of The United Methodist Church, and in the tens of millions of dollars contributed to theological education.

(24) Perhaps the most important pieces of good news include: (a) the rate of the decrease in the number of African American members has been at a slower pace than the decline in the white membership; (b) the sharp increase in the number of members of Asian ancestry; (c) the recent increase in the number of new churches organized each year; (d) the recent increase in the number of congregations reporting an average worship attendance of 500 or more from 475 in 1980 to 604 in 1994; (e) the big inventory of

seminary trained elders (the number is now more than double the 1956 total); (f) the increase in the number of persons received by Confession of Faith in 1994 (190,683) compared to 1993 (188,089); (g) the increase in average worship attendance in 1994 (3,401,468) compared to 1993 (3,394,002); (h) the continued increase in the receipts for all benevolences from $345 million in 1990 to $378 million in 1994; (i) the existence of a UM congregation in more than 2,900 of the 3,105 counties in the United States; and (j) in 1994 the net loss in membership was down to an average of only seven per hour.

What are the trends that will help identify the direction your denomination has been going?

What Is an Operational Policy?

This next discussion is limited to two types of policy statements. One is the formal written policy officially adopted by an organization. The second is the translation of several operational decisions.

For example, a congregation may formally adopt a policy statement that declares the intention to double in size in a decade. During the next year, in order to pay off a burdensome mortgage, the congregation votes to sell the west half of its two-acre site to a bank. It also decides to cut back from scheduling two different worship services on Sunday morning ("that had divided what once was one big happy family") to only one, to cut back from two weeklong vacation Bible schools every summer to one three-day session because of the shortage of volunteers, and, to save money, to eliminate all expenditures for advertising.

The official policy is to grow in numbers, but the operational policy appears to be to shrink in size.

In retrospect, it appears that over the past thirty-five years the operational policy of The United Methodist Church has been to reduce the number of congregations, to increase the number of small churches, to cut back on the number of very large churches, to withdraw from the large central cities in the North, to begin a gradual withdrawal from the North and the West, to double the number of seminary trained clergy, to concentrate on reaching and serving people born before 1945, to sharply increase the number of subsidized congregations, to reduce the number of full-time career missionaries serving on other continents, and to increase the number of people employed by annual conferences and national agencies.

While that is less than a comprehensive statement of what has happened, it does raise what this observer believes is the central issue.

Why Did That Happen?

When the overwhelming evidence supports the contention that people born after 1955 prefer either to help pioneer the founding of new churches or to attend larger congregations, why did this denomination cut back on starting new churches and sharply increase the number of smaller churches?

One response, to paraphrase a widely viewed bumper sticker, is "Stuff Happens." No one in official leadership positions wanted this to occur, "It just happened."

A second explanation is that simply is the price of being faithful and obedient to God's call. The numerical decline is a sign of faithfulness.

A third, and far more common response is to deny what has happened. While denial is widely practiced, it never is a source of creativity or renewal!

A fourth explanation, which is only one inch from denial, is that these are unrelated trends.

A fifth is to identify the villains. This is by far the most attractive alternative because the list of villains is so long. It includes the seminaries, younger generations, the bishops, the publishing house, the conference leadership, the times, the newer denominations, the new congregations, the independent churches, the automobile, television, affluence, higher education, and the fact that Jesus, the son of God, died on the cross, which proves at least that "life is unfair."

This observer offers a sixth explanation. No one is in charge. No one agency or person or board has the authority, the responsibility, and the respect to declare, "Hey, folks. That road won't take you where you want to go."

Why is no one in charge? Because the system is dysfunctional. The current organizational structure has eliminated the role of wagon master and prohibits any person, or even an ad hoc task force, from assuming that role.

Why is the system dysfunctional? Because it is organized on the basic assumption that Christian people in general, and congregational leaders in particular, cannot be trusted.

Both the Roman Catholic Church in America and The United Methodist Church have demonstrated that to build an ecclesiastical system on the medieval feudal culture of distrust, designed with vertical lines of authority, is not the way to reach the third, fourth, fifth, and sixth generations of American-born residents. That system may have been effective in reaching the recent immigrants from Europe in 1905 or the Americans born in the 1880s, but the twenty-first century will bring a severe shortage of churchgoers born before 1900.

Before looking at a few scenarios for a new millennium, it may be useful to raise a couple of dozen policy questions for those who are responsible for designing denominational structures in the United States.[1]

9.

What Questions Should Be Asked?

I f and when the decision is made to design new wineskins for the new millennium for your denomination, the people responsible for the new design will be faced with a series of fork-in-the-road policy questions. Chapter 4 identified ten earlier fork-in-the-road issues shaping the current role of several denominations.

The time has come to raise a new set of policy questions to shape the future. Agreement on the content of those questions could be a productive step in moving out of denial and into constructive planning. Here are two dozen policy questions this observer believes belong on that list. The answers to these and other policy questions can guide the process of designing the new vessel or wineskins for carrying the message. The first two questions, however, are placed first because they focus on the message to be carried. The response to these two questions should influence the design of the new wineskins more than any other factors, including tradition and the status quo.

(1) Is the Christian faith a revealed religion that was disclosed by God in the birth, ministry, death, and resurrection of Jesus Christ and in the Holy Scriptures for all generations to come? Or is

Christianity a religion that both expects and obligates each generation to reinterpret and redefine the faith?

Many believers contend that the Scriptures are clear on the central tenets of the Christian faith, but do not provide equally clear instructions on how to design a system of governance for a denomination. Are both the contents of the vessel and the design of that vessel on the agenda? Or only the design for the new wineskins?

Other believers assert that each generation is the recipient of new revelations and fresh calls to ministry. These new interpretations call for a redefinition of traditional denominational positions on both doctrine and polity.

(2) Will your denomination in the twenty-first century (a) represent a narrowly defined confessional expression of Christianity or (b) represent a highly pluralistic and theologically inclusive stance or (c) both or (d) divide and create two new denominations, one confessional and one theologically pluralistic? One representing Jerusalem and one Athens?

The basic generalization is that the broader the belief system, the higher the level of competence required of the pastor if the goals include (a) building multigenerational congregations, (b) building congregations that average more than 160 at worship, (c) reaching new generations and new immigrants through long established churches rather than the planting of hundreds of new missions annually, (d) building multicultural *and* multigenerational congregations, and (e) creating a congregational culture that places missions, evangelism, and community outreach ahead of care of the members on the list of congregational priorities.

If the goal is to create wineskins compatible with and supportive of a highly pluralistic theological position, the choice probably will be between a denomination in which at least four out of five churches report an average worship attendance of 160 or fewer or a design that calls for (a) the typical pastorate of 25 to 30 years or longer, (b) much higher standards of competence for ordination as an elder, (c) postponing ordination until the end of the fifth year of what promises to be a long, long pastorate, (d) a relatively high degree of congregational autonomy, (e) a very high level of trust in congregational leadership, (f) an elimination of the regulatory role of denominational agencies to be replaced by a high level of competence in resourcing congregations, and (g) expecting congregations to define the qualities required for ordination.

(3) Will your denomination be inclusionary or exclusionary? The fifteenth chapter of the book of Acts describes the first of hundreds of church conferences held to debate who should be kept out. More recently the bishop of the Roman Catholic Diocese of Lincoln, Nebraska, identified twelve illegitimate groups (Hemlock Society and so forth). Membership by a Catholic in that diocese in any one of those twelve groups called for excommunication. What should be the criteria for exclusion in your denomination? Should the definition of those criteria be the responsibility of the denomination? The regional judicatories. Or should congregational leaders be trusted to define those criteria?

(4) Should the ultimate control over both the message (doctrine) and the design of the vessel (polity) be lodged in an international or global headquarters (the Roman Catholic model) or in a national body or in the annual conferences or in the congregations? Or should one (the message) be lodged in the denomination and one (polity) be lodged in the congregation?

If the decision is to create a structure with the ultimate control lodged in a national (or global) body, should the constitution contain a reservation equivalent to the Tenth Amendment to the United States Constitution?

(5) Should the sense of the interdependence of the churches (connectionalism) be expressed in and through the polity (the Roman Catholic and the United Methodist models) or in that compelling vision that places evangelism and missions at the top of the agenda for both congregations and denominational agencies (the Southern Baptist model)?

(6) Should the new wineskin (the polity) be designed as a permission-withholding and controlling structure to compensate for the sinful nature of human beings? Or should it be designed as a permission-granting structure to motivate and challenge the vision and gifts of committed Christians?

In other words, should a guiding assumption be that the laity and congregational leaders cannot be trusted? Or that they can be trusted? Will the new structure be built on trust or distrust?

(7) Will the new vessel be designed so that the *primary* initiative for identifying and mobilizing the resources to meet new needs will be placed in (a) the national agencies, (b) the regional judicatories, or (c) the congregations?

(8) Where will congregations founded before 1970 be expected to look for help in redefining their identity and role as they seek to identify and serve a new constituency in the twenty-first century? The national denominational agencies? The regional judicatories? Teaching churches? Parachurch organizations? Faith-based and value-driven church affiliated hospitals? Theological schools? Private consultants? Retreat centers? Interdenominational resource centers? New pastoral leadership?

(9) Will a focus on (a) ideological concerns and institutional maintenance or (b) missions and evangelism drive the process for designing a new vessel?

One alternative is to focus the national and regional structures on evangelism and missions while trusting congregations and ad hoc single-interest groups to speak to such highly divisive issues as American foreign policy, human sexuality, the next president of the student body at the local high school, the reform of the institutions of higher education, urban renewal, the alleviation of poverty, the proportion of the state budget to be allocated to the public schools, substance abuse, vouchers, and the future of the United Nations. Unity in mission would replace polarization over divisive social, economic, and political issues as the distinctive national image of that denomination.

(10) For many Anglicans and Lutherans a driving force in the denominational decision-making process is to keep the doors open for eventual reunion with the Roman Catholic Church. Should that be a driving force in designing the new wineskins for your denomination?

For several denominations should a driving force in the new design be to facilitate implementation of the plans emerging from the Consultation on Church Union or merger with another denomination?

(11) Should the new wineskin be designed to facilitate a cutback in size or should the new design be compatible with doubling or tripling the number of members during the twenty-first century?

(12) Should the new wineskin be designed to continue to increase the number of small congregations, thus reinforcing dependency, feudal subserviency, and denominational control? Or should the new vessel be designed to encourage the emergence of more very large congregations in order to reach more people and mobilize more resources, even if that undermines dependency and control?

(13) What will be the primary role of the chief executive officer of the regional judicatory? Wagon master? Fund-raiser? Pastor to pastors? Ceremonial figure? Manager of the regional system of ministerial placement? Ecumenical relations? Leader of a team of specialists committed to helping congregations design and implement a strategy that has been custom made for that congregation? A leader and policy maker in the national offices of that denomination?

(14) Given the limitation on financial resources, should financing the regional structures be the top priority in allocating funds? Or should the top priority be given to financing the ministries of the national churchwide agencies? Or should the top priority be funding benefits for the clergy? Or should the top priority be planting new missions to reach new generations and recent immigrants?

(15) Should the design call for the congregations to raise the money to fund the regional and national structures? Or should the regional and national agencies be expected to raise money in direct contributions from individual donors, corporations, foundations, and governments, and from the sales of services not only to fund their own operations, but also to be able to challenge congregations with matching grants for new expressions of congregational outreach?

(16) Should financial subsidies from denominational funds be directed to those institutions providing the services? This was the

pattern followed by governments before 1933 in subsidizing public schools, poorhouses, mental institutions, hospitals, universities, park systems, and so forth. Or should they follow the newer pattern of Social Security, the G.I. Bill of Rights, Aid for Families with Dependent Children, food stamps, Medicare, Pell Grants, and provide the financial support to the recipient who will choose the provider of the services? For example, should the funds now sent directly to theological schools be used for scholarships for candidates for the ministry? Who should nominate the persons to receive scholarships? Congregations? Regional judicatories? National denominational agencies? The theological schools? Parents? Should the answer be the institution that has the greatest interest in the outcome of that process? Or should it be the donors of the scholarship funds?

Is this a quality question? Or a control issue? Or an issue of evangelism and missions?

(17) Who should define the criteria for ordination? Congregations? Regional judicatories? The national church? Who will be held accountable for the future consequences of the decisions on which candidates will be recommended for ordination? Who will endure the consequences of what turned out to be bad decisions? Which will be the crucial criteria for ordination? Character? The clarity of the call? Christian commitment? Competence? Academic credentials? Ability to work as a member of a staff team? Which will be the number one criterion for screening candidates?

(18) In several American Protestant traditions the theological seminaries are expected to issue a recommendation on a graduate's candidacy for ordination. That is sometimes described as a "trade school practice" that is not appropriate for a graduate school of theology. What will the new design call for on this question?

(19) Who will first closely study the strategy of that regional judicatory and subsequently examine candidates for ordination to increase the chances the candidate's qualifications are consistent with the strategy? Congregations? Regional judicatories? The theological schools?

(20) (This is a United Methodist question. Rephrase it to fit your polity, traditions, and strategy.) If the new design includes the office of bishop, will the episcopal leaders be expected to act as legislators representing the whole church —a parallel to the role of the United States senator? Or will the bishops be expected to be initiating leaders (like a governor or mayor) who will serve as chief executive officer of that regional judicatory? (A common political distinction is that legislators talk while governors and mayors lead.)

Or will bishops be expected to be ecclesiastical symbols while the leadership responsibility will be vested in a conference chief executive office? Or in a committee of volunteers? (One parallel is in municipal government. Many years ago a popular form of city government was the commission system. Part-time commissioners acted as the legislative body and also as a group executive. It is not irrelevant to note how that form of municipal government has been disappearing rapidly. The concept of a group executive has little support today.) Or will the real control be vested in those who prepare the budget for that regional judicatory?

In other words, where will their responsibility be lodged for formulating and implementing a comprehensive strategy for that regional judicatory? Or will each congregation be expected to design its own strategy? (Currently *The Book of Discipline of The United Methodist Church* severely limits a congregation's authority to prepare and implement its own unilateral strategy. The most obvious limitations are: (a) the selection of the ordained staff, (b) the comparatively short ministerial tenure of five to ten years, (c) the definition of the geographical area to be served, (d) restrictions on real estate decisions, (e) the allocation of funds for outreach and missions, and (f) mandated program and administrative agencies.)

(21) (Again, rephrase to fit your polity, traditions, and strategy.) If the new design calls for district superintendents, will their *primary* responsibility be (a) to help congregations design and implement their own strategy unilaterally or (b) to encourage congregations to design a strategy that is consistent with the larger conference strategy or (c) to encourage congregations to send money to the conference headquarters or (d) to function as an extension of the

episcopal office or (e) to serve as a legislator on conference committees or (f) to make the district an effective program agency or (g) to serve as a personnel officer or (h) to regulate congregations or (i) to be the pastor to pastors seeking pastoral care or (j) to represent the various denominational agencies and programs and seek to encourage positive congregational responses to denominational initiatives.

If the answer is "All of the above plus more," the new design should decide on a back-up system for at least eight of those ten responsibilities.

It is worth noting that the 1866 edition of *The Book of Discipline of The Methodist Episcopal Church* devotes approximately 600 words to the duties of Presiding Elders. The 1992 *Book of Discipline of The United Methodist Church* expanded this to 1,800 words. The range of duties has been greatly expanded. In 1866 the focus of the presiding elder's duties was on oversight of congregations and pastors. In 1992 a far greater emphasis on the role of the district superintendent was to serve as an officer of the annual conference, as an administrator, as a promoter of conference causes and programs, as a regulator, and as an advocate of ecumenism.

(22) In recent years pastors and congregations have become the primary building blocks for ecumenical ventures in ministry. Should that be built into the new design? Or should the design call for regional judicatories and/or national agencies once again to become the basic building blocks for new ecumenical ventures?

(23) While this really is a means-to-an-end question, which of these alternatives will be chosen for funding the national and regional agencies of your denomination in the twenty-first century, (a) designated contributions from congregations, (b) income from user fees, (c) income from investments, (d) special gifts, bequests, and other contributions from individual donors, (e) the current system, or (f) some combination of the above?

This is an extremely urgent issue since (a) the resistance in congregations to sending money to the national church appears to be growing, (b) several mainline denominations include a large number of mature members with considerable accumulated wealth, and (c) the next few decades will bring an unprecedented intergenerational transfer of wealth. The Presbyterian Church (U.S.A.) has a national foundation with over $1 billion in assets. A modest goal for your denomination would be at least $500 per confirmed member in assets in your national denomination foundation by the year 2030.

Should the new system be designed to encourage your members to remember a national denominational foundation in their wills? Should the national denominational agencies be expected to operate on the funds received from the income from investments plus user fees? Or should the system be designed to encourage members to leave their bequests to congregations, parachurch organizations, retreat centers, television ministries, state universities, annual conferences, missionary societies, church-related colleges and seminaries, and other worthy causes?

For several denominations that is a billion dollar policy decision!

10.

WHAT ARE THE SCENARIOS?

The sixty-five synods in the Evangelical Lutheran Church in America range in size from under 10,000 baptized members to slightly over 200,000. The middle one-third range between 60,000 and 99,000 baptized members. Only three include more than 150,000 baptized members. By contrast, the Southern Baptist Convention includes fifteen very large state conventions, each with more than 300,000 resident baptized members. Only two of the sixteen synods in the Presbyterian Church (U.S.A.) include more than 300,000 communicant members.

An obvious conclusion is that when the time comes to define the role of a regional judicatory, the Lutherans will come up with a different statement than will the Baptists in those fifteen very large state conventions. Likewise the Presbyterians will have to customize their definition of the role and responsibilities of a synod to match the size and resources as well as their tradition of focusing on presbyteries—but no more than 7 of the 172 presbyteries include as many as 60,000 baptized members.

How Do You Conceptualize Tomorrow?

Instead of pushing the discussions until everyone on the task force can support a specific recommendation, a process that often leads to a search for the least common denominator, a different approach calls for describing several scenarios. After each of the scenarios has been described, the next step is to identify the advantages and disadvantages of each and concurrently the changes required to transfer each scenario from a paper model to reality are listed.

For example, if it is agreed that a resident baptized membership of at least 300,000 is required for a regional judicatory to be able to mobilize the resources needed to fully resource congregations, six out of seven Southern Baptist congregations currently are affiliated with a state convention of that size or larger. Only six (Texas, North Georgia, Western North Carolina, Florida, Virginia, and West Ohio) United Methodist conferences report more than 300,000 baptized members. Thus if a scenario for the future calls for the regional judicatory to be the primary denominational agency for resourcing congregations, Lutherans, Presbyterians, and Methodists will have to look at the price tag of creating larger synods and conferences.

One alternative is to lower that bar to 150,000 resident baptized members and design a system that will enable a regional judicatory of that size to fully resource congregations.

The point of this discussion is to emphasize that detailed scenarios for the future of a particular denominational system must be customized for each denomination. This can be illustrated by looking briefly at seven different scenarios for The United Methodist Church.

Before examining these seven alternative scenarios, it should be emphasized this is far from a complete list! A strong case can be made that the doctrine of ascending liability may wipe out all denominational systems as we have known them. Many United Methodists already are on record that they prefer a merger with several other denominations that could create a new united Protestant denomination with 75,000 to 80,000 congregations. Other futurists know that the technology and the capital exists for the creation of a United Methodist Intranet that could replace the present connectional system (currently built on polity) with an electronic network designed to resource congregations with an information system that is available anywhere, anytime, and in any place.

The first of these seven requires no changes and assumes that everyone is content to see this denomination drift into oblivion rather than respond to the absence of initiating and responsible leadership.

The second, fifth, and seventh scenarios are based on a literal interpretation of *The Book of Discipline of The United Methodist Church*, which declares that the number one specific responsibility of a bishop is "to lead . . . ," and on the assumption that a connectional system based on European vertical lines of authority can be remodeled to be acceptable to (a) third, fourth, and fifth generation American-born residents, (b) people who trace their ancestry back to Africa rather than to Europe, and (c) new immigrants who have left a society built on vertical lines of authority to come to a land that they believe affirms horizontal relationships.

These three scenarios also are based on the assumption that (a) the wound inflicted on the United Methodist episcopacy in Denver in April 1996 will not prove to be fatal and (b) the current system does permit a bishop to move from being the manager of a ministerial placement system to accept a role as the leader of an annual conference.

The third scenario is based on the possibly naive assumption that *The Book of Discipline* statement, "The General Conference has full legislative power over all matters distinctively connectional," can be taken literally and also is able to exercise that power in an internally coherent and consistent manner.[1]

The fourth scenario is based on the assumption that if no one else can be trusted to lead, perhaps the time has come to trust the local leadership. This, of course, is the most radical suggestion in this book! The sixth scenario represents another hope, "Well, if no one with authority will lead, maybe some who are assigned responsibilities, but have limited authority, will step in to fill the vacuum."

The Voluntary Association

This first scenario reflects the difference between a voluntary association and a covenant community. American Methodism in the seventeenth and early-eighteenth centuries was basically a network of small, disciplined, and closely knit covenant communities with strong continuing lay leadership and occasional visits from circuit riding preachers. In recent decades most United Methodist congregations have drifted in the direction of becoming voluntary associations. One evidence of this is that on most weekends the majority of members stay away from corporate worship or go elsewhere to church.

A central component of the definition of a voluntary association is that the member retains an unrestricted right to withdraw.[2] It is far more difficult to unilaterally withdraw from a covenant community. When this distinction is combined with Robert D. Putnam's analysis of "civic disengagement," it helps to explain why this scenario has become so popular in recent years.

The discontented simply disappear. Many drop into an inactive role, but do not terminate their membership. Others go to churches that (1) help people move from inquirer to believer to member to learner to disciple to apostle and/or (2) challenge the laity to be engaged in doing ministry and/or (3) invite people to become members of a high-expectation covenant community. Others simply disappear without leaving a paper trail such as a request for a letter of transfer or a statement of withdrawal.

This is the downhill, largely ignored, smooth, and attractive path followed by more than 100,000 discontented United Methodist members every year. Many are the adult children, born in the 1940s or 1950s or 1960s or 1970s, to second, third, or fourth generation Methodist parents. A few are clergy. A significant number were reared in a Methodist or EUB parsonage.

Perhaps one-fourth of them do ask for a letter of transfer to the new church of their choice. The other three-fourths go to congregations that neither seek nor accept letters of transfer from United

Methodist congregations. Another 30,000 simply drop into inactivity as far as church is concerned.

When asked to reflect on their journey, these former UMs frequently wonder aloud about three questions no one ever asked them. "Why did you leave?" "Where did you go?" "Why this church?"

How many are choosing this scenario? Far more than any other scenario on this list! They number approximately 100,000 a year or nearly 275 a day. One-half of all United Methodist congregations claim 125 or more members. That means the equivalent of two average size congregations choose this scenario every day!

The Episcopal Initiative

A second scenario surfaced on a cold day in March when I was discussing the United Methodist withdrawal from the Midwest with a couple of midwestern pastors, one of whom is Jack Stubbs, who declared, "Lyle, I don't agree with your diagnosis, and if the diagnosis is wrong, the prescription may not be appropriate. I am convinced the central symptomatic issue is leadership. By definition, leaders accept the fact they can and should be held accountable for the future consequences of present actions. Furthermore, by definition, effective leaders accept the responsibility to take the initiative in instituting the appropriate corrective actions. We do not hold our leaders accountable, and we do not expect them to be initiating leaders."

"I couldn't agree with you more," I replied, "but in my opinion that is a product of our dysfunctional system. The present system neither expects nor permits officials to be held accountable nor to be initiating leaders. That's why we need to create a system that has built-in self-correcting components. For example, the key committee in implementing a long-range conference strategy is the conference board of ordained ministry. Their decisions should be compatible with and supportive of that conference's strategy, but if there is no conference strategy, how can they be held accountable?"

"That's a misreading of the nature of organizations," patiently explained Jack. "Effective leaders can instill in any organization both accountability and initiative. Do you understand the power of modeling?"

"Yes, I believe modeling is the most powerful pedagogical concept we know," I replied. "For example, as Christians we challenge people to model their lives after Jesus."

"Okay," continued Jack. "Instead of investing huge resources and tremendous amounts of time in replacing what you call a dysfunctional system, all that is needed is for leaders to model effective leadership."

"Let's be careful we're not preaching Pelagianism," I warned. "Don't neglect the power of original sin!"

"You're changing the subject," interrupted Jack. "Let me explain how this could be done. The first order of business on the first full day of annual conference would be the report of the conference statistician. Following that report, the bishop will stand up and declare, 'I am convinced that average worship attendance is our most sensitive and useful indicator in all of our statistical reporting. I accept full responsibility for the fact that last year for the third (seventeenth?) consecutive year the churches in this conference have experienced a decline in worship attendance. These are the three initiatives I intend to address during the next twelve months to reverse that decline. . . . The bishop would next recognize each district superintendent. One by one, each superintendent would stand and declare, 'I accept full responsibility for the continued numerical decline in my district and these are the three steps I intend to take during the next twelve months to reverse that pattern.' In several conferences an occasional superintendent would stand and explain, 'Last year, for the fourth (second?) consecutive year, our district reported an increase in worship attendance. This was largely a result of the increases in eleven of our churches. I have talked with the leaders in each of those congregations about what they did to produce that increase. As a result of those conversations, these are the three steps I plan to implement during the next twelve months to increase the number of churches in this district that will experience an increase in worship attendance!'"

"Wow!" exclaimed one of the pastors in the group. "Do you really believe that could happen?"

"Certainly!" declared Jack. "That is how leaders model accountability and initiative."

"That's an impressive scenario," I agreed, "but I have two reservations. First, if that could work, why haven't several bishops initiated that approach? My explanation is that the system diffuses authority and responsibility to such a degree that your scenario becomes impossible. Second, if we were to implement your proposal, I would want to add another component. This is based on the power of peer leadership. This would mean extending that session another hour or two. After the last superintendent had spoken, the bishop would recognize the senior pastor of a large congregation who would stand and say, 'Last year our congregation experienced a four percent decline in church attendance. It is tempting to offer excuses, but instead of doing that, I accept full responsibility. These are the three things we are planning to do that we believe will reverse that pattern.' The next pastor to be recognized would say, 'Last year, for the third consecutive year, we enjoyed at least a five percent increase in worship attendance. We are convinced this was the result of actions A, B, and C that we have taken. If any of you want to learn from our experiences, we would be glad to talk with you!' The first, third, fifth, seventh, and ninth pastors would stand, accept responsibility for the decline and explain what they planned to do to reverse that record. The second, fourth, sixth, eighth, and tenth would stand to explain their constructive actions. This would add a note of hope to the agenda and also reinforce the concept of influential peer models."

"I can buy that," agreed Jack. "The point is leadership. We need to have highly visible models of leaders affirming accountability and accepting the role of the initiating leader."

"And that takes us back to where we began," I explained. "My thesis is the present system is an environment that makes it impossible for this scenario to be played out in real life."

Jack's scenario is based on three assumptions: (a) there is a vast difference between effective leaders and good managers;[3] (b) bishops are called to be leaders, not managers; and (c) a determined bishop can enlist the allies required for transformational leadership, despite the limitations imposed by a dysfunctional organizational structure.

Do you believe this scenario is possible in the current institutional environment?

The General Conference Initiative

A modest first step toward implementing a third scenario was taken by the 1996 General Conference. This scenario calls for repealing *all* paragraphs in *The Book of Discipline* that describe and limit the role and responsibilities of an annual conference. Unfortunately, however, the 1996 General Conference took only a tiny step in this direction, and thus implementation of this scenario will require additional action by the General Conference.

To be effective or workable, this scenario requires granting each annual conference the authority to elect its own bishop (if the organizational structure chosen by that annual conference includes the episcopacy); to enlist, send, and support its own missionaries; to decide whether member congregations would be determined on a geographically defined or culturally defined basis or some other criteria; to define the criteria for ordination; to decide whether or not the system would include the office of district superintendent, and whether superintendents would be elected or appointed; to design its own system for the collection of money from congregations and other sources and the redistribution of those funds; to design its own system for the control of real estate; to create its own set of auxiliary organizations; and to design its own system for ministerial placement. The action of the 1996 General Conference grants only limited freedom to each annual conference to design its own structure.

This scenario calls for every conference to be completely free, except for changes in the Articles of Religion, to design the organizational structure it prefers.

If, for example, an annual conference decided its number one goal was to organize twenty new missions annually, that conference would be free to design a structure to accomplish that goal. If another annual conference decided its number one goal was to enhance the array of benefits available to ministers (pensions, sabbaticals, salaries, vacations, continuing education experiences), it would be free to design an organizational system to attain that goal. If another annual conference decided it wanted to encourage every congregation to become a high-commitment church filled with deeply committed disciples and apostles, it would be free to adopt an organizational structure designed to accomplish that goal. Another nongeographical annual conference could consist of congregations that want to make issues of social justice the number one priority.

This scenario is based on seven crucial assumptions: (1) local leadership can be trusted fully; (2) an effective means of evoking creativity is by challenging people; (3) people can and will learn when they have to live with the future consequences of present actions; (4) conference leaders are open and eager to learn from the relevant experiences of others; (5) horizontal relationships are more compatible with the contemporary American culture than are vertical lines of authority; (6) locally formulated goals are more likely to attract widespread support than are goals imposed from above; and (7) the distinctive connectional thread should be carried in the Articles of Religion, rather than in the polity.

The Free Market Shuffle

A fourth scenario represents an expansion of the third. This carries the level of trust to a far greater extent. Instead of simply trusting the conference leadership to custom design an organizational structure for that annual conference, this scenario goes a giant step beyond that. This scenario is based on the assumption that congregational leaders can be trusted! That requires a reversal of the trend in this denomination in recent decades. If the conclusion is yes, congregational leaders can be trusted, that opens the door to the most radical alternative of all.

With only a half dozen restrictions, every congregation would be free to help design and become a member of the annual conference of its choice. For example, several score congregations in the metropolitan Kansas City area could come together to create a geographically defined annual conference serving that bi-state community. Several score African American congregations could come together and create a nongeographical annual conference. A few hundred rural and small town churches in the Great Plains could create an annual conference designed to resource rural and small town churches. Two hundred of the 475 congregations currently averaging 500 or more at worship could come together to create a nongeographical annual conference of large churches. A couple of nongeographical annual conferences could be organized around social justice issues. Several others could be organized as "confessional conferences" while others could choose theological pluralism as their distinctive identity.

This scenario would challenge the creativity of local leaders. They would be free to design an annual conference that would reflect their needs, their ideological convictions, their theological stance, and their vision of the Christian church in the twenty-first century. This would strengthen the horizontal lines from congregation to congregation.

The obvious first restriction would be that any congregation that chose to become an independent church would be free to do so, but they would offer to surrender title to the real estate and other assets, including the name, to the trustees of The United Methodist Church.

The second restriction would forbid any tampering with the Articles of Religion.

A third restriction would be that any congregation that chose to play a passive "wait and see" game would be admitted to the annual conference of its eventual choice only on approval of two-thirds of the voting delegates of that new annual conference. This would encourage, but not require, every congregation to accept an active initiating role in creating the new annual conferences. Congregations that could not attain that two-thirds approval vote of the nongeographical conference of its choice or declared no preference would automatically be placed in the appropriate geographical conference.

A fourth restriction would be that these decisions would be binding for ten (eight? twelve?) years. A congregation would not be permitted to switch from one conference to another except once every ten years. Every ten years this free market shuffle would be repeated. The only exceptions would be if a congregation could both (a) secure permission by a two-thirds vote to leave its annual conference and (b) secure by a two-thirds vote an invitation from the conference of its choice.

Fifth, every proposed annual conference would be required to include at least (a) 50,000 church members or (b) 200 congregations.

Finally, every annual conference would be required to accept the credentials of any minister in good standing in another annual conference if a congregation in the conference seeking the services of that minister asks for the transfer of ministerial standing. This would be necessary to facilitate an otherwise unrestricted national ministerial placement pool.

The possibility that one or more congregations could choose to terminate its relationship with a particular conference once every ten years without a permission-granting vote would enhance the sensitivity of conference "headquarters" to the concerns of the churches. The two-thirds vote for admission would be an inducement to those churches that had earned a reputation of "noncooperative" or "troublemakers" to mend their ways.

After their formal organization, representations of these new annual conferences would gather to create what they perceived to be the necessary regional and/or national organizational structures.

This could be the ultimate expression of the "bottoms up" approach to restructure and would institutionalize the conviction that local leaders can and should be trusted. In recent years the Methodist Church in Korea and the Free Methodist Church in Canada have completed radical restructuring efforts. Both were based on the assumption that local leadership can be trusted.

Those readers who are convinced this is a completely unworkable alternative need to be reminded that this is the approach that was used originally to create most of what today are identified as American Protestant denominations. They did it without the advantages of airplanes, automobiles, paved roads, telephones, fax machines, E-mail, videotapes, motel rooms, and consultants!

The Blue-Ribbon Committee

This book was written with the expectation that the most conservative of these seven scenarios will be chosen. To be more specific, a fifth scenario calls for someone (General Conference, the Council of Bishops, a gathering of council directors, a couple of dozen annual conferences) to call for the creation of a blue-ribbon committee of seven to fifteen respected, knowledgeable, future-oriented, open, wise, and thoughtful individuals to design a recommended organizational structure for this denomination for the beginning of the third millennium. They would be given (1) the Articles of Religion, (2) a blank sheet of paper, and (3) a vote of confidence and instructed to do the job.

This book was written to raise a few of the questions and to articulate a few of the issues that this blue-ribbon committee would have to confront. At this writing it is impossible to discern whether the new Connectional Process Team will be free to suggest radical changes or will be limited to redesigning the present system.

The Number One Stakeholders

The sixth of these seven scenarios is based on the assumption that the people most directly concerned about the future of this denomination in general and the annual conferences in particular are the council directors. As a group they really have only five choices: (a) learn to live with ambiguity and frustration; (b) relax and enjoy a personal hobby; (c) look forward to retirement; (d) seek another line of work; or (e) come together and accept the role of reformers.

One alternative would be to come together and create a blue-ribbon committee similar to what is described in the fifth scenario. Another would be to adopt a tentative design that each council director would bring back to his or her annual conference for revisions and support. Ideally, by early 1999 agreement would be secured on a common denomination-wide basic design, and most of the delegates elected at the 1999 annual conferences to serve in the General Conference of 2000 would be committed to support that design. This would place the power to initiate radical changes in the annual conferences.

A more conservative, and far less complicated alternative would be for the council directors to seek to persuade the General Council on Finance and Administration to add a program budget to their report to the General Conference of 2000.

The traditional set of tables would describe who will receive how many dollars in each year of the new quadrennium.

The additional table would be a program budget that focuses on outcomes rather than inputs. This approach to budgeting has been widely used for many decades by local governments, nonprofit corporations, profit-making companies, and congregations. A simple congregational expression of this approach to budgeting divides all proposed expenditures among three categories.[4]

   I. Ministries to and with members.
  II. Community ministries beyond the membership including evangelism.
 III. Ministries beyond this community.

All proposed expenditures for staff compensation, real estate, utilities, benevolences, postage, are divided so that the appropriate amount is allocated to each of these three categories.

What would a program budget for The United Methodist Church look like if limited to the annual conferences and general agencies, exclusive of the General Board of Pensions and The United Methodist

Publishing House? Here are a few of the categories that could be used with the estimated combined annual expenditures by annual conferences and general agencies, based on 1995 expenditures.

Planting new churches to reach the unchurched, younger, generations, and recent immigrants	$12 million
Support of career UM missionaries outside USA	$? million
Resourcing congregations (excludes ministerial placement)	$25 million
Operation of the appointment system of ministerial placement	$30 million
Producing 500 new elders annually	$12 million
Litigation	$ 2 million
Scholarships	$? million
Direct and indirect financial subsidies to congregations	$12.5 million
Collecting and redistributing money (administrative costs)	$? million
Pastoral care of pastors	$15 million
Grants by the General Board of Global Ministries to entities not formally part of the UMC	$11.1 million

It should be emphasized that these are (a) illustrative categories, (b) estimates of expenditures, and (c) far from a complete list of categories. The point is to focus on performance or outcomes, not on who receives the money. This would enable the General Conference to make better informed decisions on policy questions.

Given the growing shortage of funds for both the annual conferences and the general agencies, a program or performance budget could be a useful means of clarifying the financial costs of alternative courses of action.

The Aldersgate Scenario

The Council of Bishops schedules a three-day retreat with an agenda restricted to fasting, confession, reflection, prayer, Bible study, worship, and sharing. Attendance is limited solely to currently active bishops. On the morning of the first day, the bishops arrive at the Aldersgate Retreat Center. The schedule includes a three-hour period of time together on both the first and second evenings. The last half of the first evening, that time is devoted to a worship service centered on Holy Communion. The bishop who preached at that service uses Acts 2 as the text.

The evening session for the second day is held in a large plain room with a huge fireplace and a roaring fire as the only source of heat on that chilly fall evening. After two hours of prayer, singing, and reflections, one of the bishops holds up a copy of this book, walks over to the fireplace, tosses the book in, and, as the fire eagerly consumes the dry pages, declares, "This book has got it all wrong! Our problem is not a dysfunctional organizational structure. Our problem is we've lost our passion for evangelism."

As the bishop-turned-exhorter continues for another thirty minutes, the room is filled with nods of agreement, many hearts are strangely warmed, and there are scattered cries of, "Amen!" "Preach!" and "Right on!" That session, which was scheduled to conclude with a devotional time and be over by ten o'clock, continued until nearly two in the morning.

In the middle of the next afternoon, the bishops leave to go home to lead a spiritual revival that transforms two-thirds of the existing congregations and launches ten thousand new congregations over the next two decades.

In the year 2138, a minister, in what now is called simply The Methodist Church, writes a ten-page essay. The first couple of pages laments the numerical decline of the American branch of this religious tradition from a peak of 33 million members scattered among 80,000 congregations in the year 2090 to fewer than 25 million in 70,000 congregations in 2137. Members lost by death outnumber the new converts.

The final six sentences of that essay read as follows.

"Four hundred years ago, a new religious revival began at a place called Aldersgate. It spread beyond the confines of the Anglican tradition. The history of that movement suggested that new wineskins are required to carry the gospel to new generations. About a hundred and forty years ago, however, another new revival began in another place also called Aldersgate. The history of that reawakening suggests that God can use old systems, which some in that day called dysfunctional, to launch a new religious reawakening. I wonder if it can happen again in the world we are living in today?"

APPENDIX:TABLES

Table I
The Changing Ecclesiastical Landscape

Denomination	1968*		1994*	
	No. of Congreg.	Inclusive Mbship	No. of Congreg.	Inclusive Mbship
AME Zion	4,500	870,421	3,098	1,230,842
Am. Baptist Conv.	5,968	1,454,965	5,686	1,507,934
Assemblies of God	8,570	626,660	11,764	2,324,615
Baptist Gen'l Conf.	591	100,000	813	135,128
Chr. & Missionary All.	1,128	119,826	1,943	302,414
Chr. Church (Disciples)	5,862	1,592,609	3,933	937,644
CME Church	2,598	466,718	2,340	718,922
Chr. Reformed Church	648	281,523	737	211,154
Ch. of God (Anderson)	2,265	146,807	2,314	216,117
Ch. of God (Cleveland)	3,834	243,532	5,918	722,541
LDS (Mormons)	4,517	2,180,064	10,218	4,613,000
Ch. of Brethren	1,054	187,957	1,127	144,282
Ch. of Nazarene	4,674	364,789	5,156	597,841
Episcopal Church	7,137	3,373,890	7,388	2,504,682
Evang. Covenant Ch.	514	66,021	597	89,511
Evang. Free Church	539	59,041	1,213	227,290
Ev. Luth. Ch. in Am.	N.A.	N.A.	10,973	5,199,048

Denomination	1968* No. of Congreg.	Inclusive Mbship	1994* No. of Congreg.	Inclusive Mbship
Jehovah's Witnesses	5,341	333,672	10,307	945,900
Luth. Ch.- Mo. Synod	5,733	2,781,892	6,148	2,596,927
Pentecostal Assemblies	500	45,000	1,760	1,000,000
Presbyterian Ch.(USA)	12,176	4,184,430	11,399	3,698,136
Prog.Natl.Bapt.Conv.Inc.	655	521,692	2,000	2,500,000
Reformed Church in Am.	939	383,166	915	309,459
Roman Catholic Church	23,781	47,873,238	19,723	60,190,605
Seventh Day Adv.	3,202	396,097	4,303	775,349
Southern Bapt. Conv.	34,275	11,330,481	39,863	15,614,060
United Ch. of Christ	6,866	2,032,648	6,180	1,501,310
United Methodist Ch.	41,901	10,990,720	36,559	8,584,125
U. Pentecostal Ch.Int.	2,500	225,000	3,730	550,000
Wesleyan Church	2,559	82,358	1,609	116,763
Wisc. Ev. Luth. Synod	869	358,466	1,251	414,874

*In several cases the first year was 1967 or 1969 and in the last column the reporting year was 1993.
Sources: *Yearbook of American Churches 1970.*
Yearbook of American and Canadian Churches 1996.

Table II
United Methodist Membership by States

States	1960 Methodist and E.U.B. Membership	1990 UMC Membership	1960 E.U.B. and Methodist Percent of Population	1990 UMC Membership Percent of Population
Alabama	314,413	264,968	9.62	6.56
Alaska	3,145	3,712	1.39	0.67
Arizona	35,100	47,008	2.70	1.28
Arkansas	181,627	156,962	10.17	6.68
California	324,367	210,395	2.06	0.70
Colorado	93,785	72,042	5.35	2.18
Connecticut	52,323	46,214	2.06	1.41
Delaware	46,866	49,118	10.50	7.38

States	1960 Methodist and E.U.B. Membership	1990 UMC Membership	1960 E.U.B. and Methodist Percent of Population	1990 UMC Membership Percent of Population
Dist. of Columbia	35,710	15,506	4.67	2.56
Florida	270,236	380,963	5.46	2.95
Georgia	378,668	418,835	9.60	6.46
Hawaii	4,644	6,677	0.73	0.60
Idaho	21,380	16,008	3.20	1.50
Illinois	532,708	351,260	5.28	3.07
Indiana	425,425	272,999	9.12	4.92
Iowa	313,078	216,489	11.35	7.80
Kansas	267,305	187,473	12.27	7.57
Kentucky	206,499	182,302	6.80	4.94
Louisiana	140,116	133,256	4.30	3.16
Maine	33,857	29,043	3.49	2.36
Maryland	256,755	250,056	8.28	5.23
Massachusetts	100,823	58,929	1.96	0.97
Michigan	303,599	199,321	3.88	2.14
Minnesota	136,839	112,200	4.01	2.56
Mississippi	220,228	186,445	10.11	7.24
Missouri	275,394	203,787	6.38	4.98
Montana	28,918	15,186	4.29	1.90
Nebraska	140,970	114,289	9.99	7.24
Nevada	5,230	6,835	1.83	0.57
New Hampshire	17,849	15,469	2.94	1.39
New Jersey	192,601	134,996	3.17	1.75
New Mexico	52,077	41,920	5.48	2.77
New York	485,320	376,410	2.89	2.09
North Carolina	464,692	491,742	10.20	7.41
North Dakota	26,115	18,781	4.13	2.94
Ohio	748,706	521,445	7.71	4.80
Oklahoma	252,929	258,209	10.86	8.21
Oregon	63,933	33,607	3.61	1.18
Pennsylvania	771,313	588,732	6.81	4.95
Rhode Island	9,604	7,748	1.12	0.77
South Carolina	230,364	244,591	9.67	7.01
South Dakota	44,631	33,703	6.56	4.84
Tennessee	376,901	320,724	10.57	6.58
Texas	764,587	781,389	7.98	4.60
Utah	4,500	4,598	0.51	0.26

States	1960 Methodist and E.U.B. Membership	1990 UMC Membership	1960 E.U.B. and Methodist Percent of Population	1990 UMC Membership Percent of Population
Vermont	24,397	19,520	6.26	3.47
Virginia	425,011	398,191	10.71	6.43
Washington	90,177	70,644	3.16	1.45
West Virginia	252,020	148,712	13.55	8.29
Wisconsin	151,073	120,304	3.82	2.46
Wyoming	13,911	10,090	4.21	2.22

Sources: 1960 statistics from *General Minutes, 1972*, p. 28.
1990 membership figures from *Churches and Church Membership in the United States 1990* (Atlanta: Glenmary Research Center, 1992), pp. 12-36.

Table III
Annual Death Rates
Death per 1000 Persons

1952	U.S.A. (Population age 14 and over)	11.8
1970	U.S.A. (Population age 14 and over)	12.2
1994	U.S.A. (Population age 14 and over)	10.7
1952	Methodist Church	8.9
1952	E.U.B. Church	10.7
1964	Methodist Church	7.4
1966	E.U.B. Church	12.0
1970	United Methodist Church	10.4
1980	United Methodist Church	12.6
1994	United Methodist Church	14.2
1994	Presbyterian Church in America	7.4
1993	Evangelical Lutheran Church in America	12.0
1993	Lutheran Church-Missouri Synod	9.0
1994	Presbyterian Church (U.S.A.)	15.2

Table IV
Distribution of Very Large UM Churches
Average Worship Attendance of 500 or More

	*1965**	*1980*	*1994*
North Central Jurisdiction	193	97	84
Northeastern Jurisdiction	94	31	37
South Central Jurisdiction	164	129	179
Southeastern Jurisdiction	189	178	259
Western Jurisdiction	107	40	45
Total	747	475	604

The 1965 totals are larger than stated here because several larger congregations did not report their average worship attendance. Central Jurisdiction churches are included in the geographical jurisdictions. The 1965 figures also do not include the large EUB churches.

Table V
Distribution of Larger UM Churches
Average Worship Attendance of 200 or More

	*1972**	*1980*	*1994*
North Central Jurisdiction	1189	1154	956
Northeastern Jurisdiction	721	659	554
South Central Jurisdiction	795	779	779
Southeastern Jurisdiction	1217	1236	1314
Western Jurisdiction	299	324	313
Totals	4221	4152	3936

*This was the first year these totals were summarized in *The General Minutes*.

Table VI
The Distribution of Small UM Churches
Reporting an Average of Fewer Than 35 at Worship

	*1972**	*1980*	*1994*
North Central Jurisdiction	1,599	1,637	2,116
Northeastern Jurisdiction	2,290	2,284	2,649
South Central Jurisdiction	2,129	2,150	2,356
Southeastern Jurisdiction	3,283	3,542	4,320
Western Jurisdiction	330	284	323
Total	9,631	9,897	11,764

*This was the first year these totals were summarized in *The General Minutes*.
Total number of congregations reporting average worship attendance:

    1972 = 36,641   1980 = 37,300   1994 = 36,521

Proportion of reporting congregations reporting an average worship attendance of fewer than 35:

    1972 = 25.6%   1980 = 26.5%   1994 = 32.3%

Table VII
Percentage of Congregations Reporting Average Worship
Attendance of 200 or More
1994

Assemblies of God	15%
Church of the Brethren	6%
Church of the Nazarene	10%
Christian Church (Disciples of Christ)	7%
Evangelical Covenant Church	25%
Evangelical Free Church	28%
Evangelical Lutheran Church in America	21%
Free Methodist Church	8.5%
Lutheran Church-Missouri Synod	28%
Presbyterian Church (U.S.A.)	16%
Reformed Church in America	28%
Southern Baptist Convention	15%
United Church of Christ	7%
United Methodist Church	11%
Wesleyan Church	9%
Wisconsin Evangelical Lutheran Synod	14%

Table VIII
Median Size of Congregations by Denomination, as Measured by Average Worship Attendance
1994

Assemblies of God	70
Church of the Brethren	58
Church of the Nazarene	65
Christian Church (Disciples of Christ)	75
Evangelical Covenant Church	98
Evangelical Free Church	115
Evangelical Lutheran Church in America	101
Free Methodist Church	55
Lutheran Church-Missouri Synod	124
Presbyterian Church (U.S.A.)	75
Reformed Church in America	114
Southern Baptist Convention	71
United Church of Christ	72
United Methodist Church	58
Wesleyan Church	56
Wisconsin Evangelical Lutheran Synod	92

Table IX
Proportion of Congregations Reporting an Average Worship Attendance of Fewer Than 20
1994

Assemblies of God	7%
Church of the Brethren	9%
Church of the Nazarene	7%
Christian Church (Disciples of Christ)	4%
Evangelical Covenant Church	3%
Evangelical Free Church	1%
Evangelical Lutheran Church in America	3%
Free Methodist Church	9%
Lutheran Church-Missouri Synod	N.A.
Presbyterian Church (U.S.A.)	8%
Reformed Church in America	2%
Southern Baptist Convention	6%
United Church of Christ	5%

United Methodist Church	15%
Wesleyan Church	6%
Wisconsin Evangelical Lutheran Synod	4%

Table X
Where Will We Find 25,000 Worshipers
on a Typical Weekend? In:

The 3 largest independent congregations
The 4 largest Assemblies of God congregations
The 5 largest Southern Baptist congregations
The 9 largest Evangelical Lutheran Church in America parishes
The 9 largest United Methodist congregations
The 10 largest Presbyterian Church (U.S.A.) congregations
The 12 largest Evangelical Free Church in America congregations
The 18 largest Reformed Church in America congregations
The 32 largest Wisconsin Evangelical Lutheran Synod congregations
The 403 smallest Reformed Church in America congregations
The 446 smallest Evangelical Free Church congregations
The 550 smallest Wisconsin Evangelical Lutheran Synod congregations
The 979 smallest Evangelical Lutheran Church in America parishes
The 1,404 smallest Presbyterian Church (U.S.A.) congregations
The 1,585 smallest Assemblies of God congregations
The 1,905 smallest Southern Baptist congregations
The 2,690 smallest United Methodist congregations

NOTES

Introduction

1. Warren Bennis, "The Leader as Storyteller," *Harvard Business Review* (January-February, 1996), p. 154.

2. Roger Finke and Rodney Stark, *The Churching of America 1776–1990* (New Brunswick, N.J.: Rutgers University Press, 1992).

1. Have You Felt the Earthquake?

1. The earthquake shaking the foundations of American-style capitalism is described by Lester Thurow, *The Future of Capitalism* (New York: William Morrow & Co., 1996). The earthquake shaking the foundations of the American political system is described by Haynes Johnson and David S. Broder, *The System: The American Way of Politics at the Breaking Point* (Boston: Little, Brown & Company, 1996). Both books are useful for understanding the larger context behind the current wave of antidenominationalism in the United States.

2. Two superb essays on the current divisions of the theological spectrum are Roger E. Olson, "Postconservative Evangelicals Greet the Postmodern Age," *The Christian Century* (May 3, 1996), pp. 480-83, and Roger E. Olson, "Back to the Bible (Almost)," *Christianity Today* (May 20, 1996), pp. 31-34.

3. The multisite and off-campus church model is described in Lyle E. Schaller, *Innovations in Ministry* (Nashville: Abingdon Press, 1994), pp. 86-133.

2. Has Your Church Felt the Earthquake?

1. For suggestions on the relocation process, see Lyle E. Schaller, *Choices for Churches* (Nashville: Abingdon Press, 1990), pp. 97-121.

3. Can We Learn from the Competition?

1. For an excellent essay on the natural tendency of a denomination to drift into a regulatory role, see Craig Dystra and James Hudnut-Beumler, "The National Organizational Structures of Protestant Denominations: An Invitation to a Conversation," Milton J. Coalter, et al., editors, *The Organizational Revolution* (Louisville: Westminster/John Knox Press, 1992), pp. 307-31. It is not irrelevant to note that one predecessor of what now is *The Book of Discipline of The United Methodist Church* was titled *Doctrines and Discipline of the Methodist Episcopal Church South.*

2. For another application of this distinction, see James Fallows, *Breaking the News* (New York: Pantheon Books, 1996), chapters 2 and 4. Fallows (p. 4) makes two other points that are relevant to this discussion. "The big American institutions that have failed in the recent past often wasted years blaming others for their problems . . . . But the larger truth is that these institutions reversed their decline only when they recognized and corrected defeats in their internal values."

3. The concept of long pastorates is not new. Between 1680 and 1750 the average length of a pastorate in the colonial churches of New England was approximately 26 years. Four out of five ministers served only one congregation in their entire career. J. William T. Youngs, Jr., *God's Messengers* (Baltimore, Md.: The Johns Hopkins University Press, 1976).

4. For an elaboration of this point, see Lyle E. Schaller, *Looking in the Mirror* (Nashville: Abingdon Press, 1984), pp. 59-88. For a powerful trinitarian brief and an attack on contemporary gnosticism, see Carl E. Braten and Robert W. Jensen, editors, *Either/Or: The Gospel of Neopaganism* (Grand Rapids, Mich.: Eerdmans, 1996).

5. Robert D. Putnam, "Tuning In, Tuning Out: The Strange Disappearance of Social Capital in America," *PS Political Science and Politics* 28/4 (December 1995), pp. 664-83. One scholar argues that centralization and hierarchy are the two great restraints on modern democracy. Robert E. Wiebe, *Self Rule: A Cultural History of American Democracy* (Chicago: University of Chicago Press, 1996).

4. What's Ahead for Your Denomination?

1. J. S. Ninomiya, "Wagon Masters and Lesser Managers," *Harvard Business Review* (March/April 1988), pp. 84-90.

2. Robert D. Putnam, *Making Democracy Work: Civic Traditions in Modern Italy* (Princeton, N.J.: Princeton University Press, 1994).

3. For an excellent essay on the nature of voluntary associations, see Lon L. Fuller, "Two Principles of Human Associations," J. Roland Pennock and John W. Chapman, editors. *Voluntary Associations* (New York: Atherton Press, 1969), pp. 3-23.

4. John R. Searle, *The Construction of Social Reality* (New York: Free Press, 1995), p. 117. An exceptionally moving, and only slightly nostalgic, account of the trade-offs in favor of choice that have undermined community and the former trust of local institutions is Alan Ehrenhalt, *The Lost City* (New York: Basic Books, 1995).

5. Francis Fukuyama, *Trust* (New York: The Free Press, 1996).

6. A. Gregory Schneider, *The Way of the Cross Leads Home* (Bloomington, Ind.: Indiana University Press, 1993), p. 200.

7. Ibid., p. 201.

8. For a readable account of the revolution in professional baseball, see John Helyer, *Lords of the Realm* (New York: Ballantine Books, 1994).

9. My thinking in this section was stimulated by the reading of an essay by Alan Wolfe, "The Feudal Culture of the Postmodern University," *The Wilson Quarterly* (Winter 1996), pp. 54-66.

10. Carolly Erickson, *The Medieval Vision* (New York: Oxford University Press, 1976), pp. 55-58.

11. For reflections on the contemporary Americanization of a European religious tradition, see Harvey A. Smit, "How Our Past Can Shape Our Future," *The Banner* (May 13, 1996), p. 4. For a revealing account of the Americanization of a congregation founded on a powerful Dutch heritage, see Elton J. Bruins, *The Americanization of the Congregation* (Grand Rapids, Mich.: Eerdmans, 1995).

12. For this discussion I am indebted to a superb essay by James Nuechterlein, "Athens and Jerusalem in Indiana," *The American Scholar* (Summer 1988), pp. 353-68. Also see George M. Marsden, *The Soul of the American University* (New York: Oxford University Press, 1994), pp. 267-91.

13. W. Clark Gilpin, "The Theological Schools: Transmission, Transformation and Transcendence of Denominational Culture," Jackson Carroll and Wade Clark Roof, editors, *Beyond Establishment* (Louisville: Westminster/John Knox Press, 1993), pp. 188-204.

5. What's It All About?

1. For a brief on behalf of the servant leader, see Robert K. Greenleaf, *Seeker and Servant: Reflections on Religious Leadership*, edited by Anne T. Fraker and Larry C. Spears (San Francisco: Jossey-Bass Publishers, 1996).

2. Stanley Pogrow, "Reforming the Wannabe Reformers," *Phi Delta Kappan* (June 1996), pp. 656-63.

3. For an impressive description of designing the ministry of a downtown church for a new era, see Howard Edington, *The Downtown Church: The Heart of the City* (Nashville: Abingdon Press, 1996).

6. What Are the Best Strategies?

1. For suggestions on this, see Lyle E. Schaller, *Strategies for Change* (Nashville: Abingdon Press, 1993).

2. A dramatic example of this is the Episcopal Diocese of Texas, which has defined unchurched people as the number one client of the diocese, rather than the clergy and the parishes. The Diocese also is building a partnership with congregational leaders to double the membership in a decade.

3. The pioneering book on learning communities is Peter M. Senge, *The Fifth Discipline* (New York: Currency Doubleday, 1990).

4. For a description of the Minister of Missions, see Lyle E. Schaller, *Innovations in Ministry* (Nashville: Abingdon Press, 1994), pp. 70-105.

7. What Are the Trade-Offs?

1. A brief and lucid summary of that polarizing debate on United Methodism is Charles A. Sayre, "The Defining Point," *Circuit Rider* (March 1996), pp. 20-21.

2. See Lyle E. Schaller, *The Small Membership Church* (Nashville: Abingdon Press, 1994), pp. 23-29.

8. What Is Contemporary Reality?

1. This is not the first book to raise questions about the future of this denomination. Earlier warnings were given by Richard B. Wilke, *Are We Yet Alive?* (Nashville: Abingdon Press, 1986); William H. Willimon and Robert L. Wilson, *Rekindling the Flame* (Nashville: Abingdon Press, 1987); Douglas W. Johnson & Alan K. Waltz, *Facts and Possibilities* (Nashville: Abingdon Press, 1987); Wade Clark Roof and William McKinney, *American Mainline Religion* (New Brunswick, N.J.: Rutgers University Press, 1987); David A. Roozen and C. Kirk Hadaway, editors, *Church and Denominational Growth* (Nashville: Abingdon Press, 1993); William Easum, *Dancing with Dinosaurs* (Nashville: Abingdon Press, 1993); and Andy Langford and William H. Willimon, *A New Connection* (Nashville: Abingdon Press, 1995).

Cutting down trees for new books may not be the best strategy for combating denominational denial. An excellent and exportable strategy for renewal is explained in Michael Slaughter, *Spiritual Entrepreneurs: Six Principles for Risking*

Notes

Renewal (Nashville: Abingdon Press, 1994). Perhaps that should be one of the two books for required reading by anyone interested in denominational renewal. The other, which should be required reading for anyone designing a new ecclesiastical system, is Edgar R. Trexler, *Anatomy of a Merger* (Minneapolis: Augsburg Fortress, 1991). This is a fascinating account written from an insider's perspective of the seven-year effort to create a new denomination for a new era by merging three Lutheran bodies into one. Trexler's account also describes many of the unexpected price tags on that effort. With a remarkable degree of candor, Trexler describes the struggle over the criteria to secure a "representative" collection of people to serve on the Commission for a New Lutheran Church. A third extremely useful book is Alan C. Klass, *In Search of the Unchurched* (Bethesda, Md.: The Alban Institute, 1996).

Instead of looking at measurable statistical trends, one scholar has suggested a sequential historical perspective and has described five stages of denominational styles in the United States. The first was the voluntary association. The second was the missionary association. The third was the "churchly" style. The fourth was the corporate or managerial style. The fifth and most recent emerged in the 1960s as the regulatory body. Russell E. Richey, "Denominations and Denominationalism: An American Morphology," in Robert Bruce Mullen and Russell E. Richey, Ed. *Reimagining Denominationalism* (New York: Oxford University Press, 1994), p. 77. American Methodism has evolved from a missionary movement in the 1784–1819 era into the contemporary regulatory role. The greater the distrust of local leadership, the greater the self-identified need by the regulators for more regulation.

10. What Are the Scenarios?

1. In one decision, the 1996 General Conference granted each United Methodist congregation additional authority in designing its own congregational structure. In another decision it required each congregation to have a local unit of the United Methodist Men and a local unit of the United Methodist Women. This is in a denomination in which 40 percent of all congregations report an average worship attendance of 40 or fewer!

2. See Lon Fuller, "Two Principles of Human Association."

3. A useful book on this distinction is Warren Bennis and Burt Nanus, *Leaders* (New York: Harper & Row, 1985).

4. The program budget is described in Lyle E. Schaller, *Parish Planning* (Nashville: Abingdon Press, 1971), pp. 36-63.